LOTHIAN

LOTHIAN

General Editor:

DAVID COLLEDGE

Contributors:

DAVID ANGUS • **THOMAS DALE** • **BASIL SKINNER** • **ROBERT SHANKS**

Designed and illustrated by:

JOHN DUGAN AND WALTER CUTHILL

HOLMES McDOUGALL EDINBURGH

SBN 7157 1928-9

Acknowledgements

Michael Courtney, Photographer
Robert Matthew, Johnston-Marshall and Partners
The Scottish Field
The Scotsman Publications Ltd.
The Farmers' Weekly
The Luing Cattle Society Ltd.
The Forth Ports Authority
Microwave and Electronic Systems Ltd.
Hewlett Packard Ltd.
Scottish and Newcastle Breweries Ltd.
The National Coal Board
Edinburgh Airport Authority
Livingston Development Corporation
The Festival Society
The Scottish Arts Council
The Controllers of Her Majesty's Stationery Office
The Royal Commission on Ancient and Historic Monuments
The Department of the Environment
The National Trust for Scotland
The National Gallery of Scotland

CONTENTS

LOTHIAN HERITAGE

CHAPTER 1

THE LAND OF LOTHIAN

The "Land of Lothian" is a semi-mythological kingdom, and for that very reason immediately takes hold of the imagination. It may, at one time, have stretched from the Forth to the Tweed along the East Coast. Certainly, there are prehistoric remains which point to a pre-Roman civilization; on the highest of the West Lothian Hills, Cairnpapple, there is evidence of a Neolithic sanctuary remodelled in the early Bronze Age (*c.* 1800 B.C.).

THE COMING OF THE ROMANS

"Lothian" is traditionally derived from King Loth, grandfather of Saint Mungo, and both are thought to come from the Gaelic word "Lattach" meaning clay. When the first Roman expeditionary force penetrated Lothian under the command of Agricola, the region was inhabited by the Votadini. Of this people little is known but they appear to have collaborated with the Roman force against the neighbouring

King Loth

Selgovae and Novantae.

There are several traces of the Roman influence in the region. Roman pottery, contemporary with Agricola's advance north, has been found in the famous hill fort at Traprain Law. Almost large enough to be a town, it was inhabited by the Votadini and was untouched by the Romans. A Roman road follows the western boundaries of the Votadini; from Corbridge to the forts at Newstead and Inveresk. The Treasure of Traprain, buried at the beginning of the 5th century A.D. and unearthed in 1919 can be seen in the

Scottish National Museum of Antiquities in Edinburgh. This hoard of silver was most likely looted from the Roman villas and churches in Gaul and buried in the hill by Saxon or Frisian pirates. A legionary tablet of great interest is also to be seen in the Museum of National Antiquities. Discovered in 1868 at Bridgeness, near Bo'ness, it was a stone set up to the Emperor Titus Antoninus Caesar who is, perhaps, best known for his ordering of the construction of the Antonine Wall, carried on by his regional governor Lullius Urbicus in 142 A.D.

The eastern extremity of the Wall was begun in present-day Carriden and stretched westwards towards the Clyde for 37 miles. 14 feet (4·3 m) wide, and built from blocks of turf, it rested on a stone bed 10 or 12 feet (3–3·7 m) high. The Wall east of Falkirk consists solely of earth. On the outside, a dry ditch was dug and a garrison placed at 2 mile (3 km) intervals along the wall making 19 in all. Running from the eastern end of the wall at Carriden was a road which carried troops and supplies to the fortress-garrison at Cramond.

It is important to point out that Scotland was never completely subjugated by the Romans, and that the Roman presence in Lothian, although lasting for well over 300 years, was in the nature of an auxiliary military outpost. Thus these Romans did not have the insidious civilizing influence of their brethren in the settlements of the South. When, in 410 A.D., Honorius told the leading citizens of Britain to manage their own affairs, Roman and British legions had already been withdrawn to fight on the continent. They never returned.

Britain's official connection with Rome ended, finally, in 410, though Vortigern maintained the Roman framework and civilization till 442.

Picts, Scots and Saxons gradually overwhelmed the Romano–British civilization: "To Aetius, thrice consul, the groans of the Britons . . . the barbarians drive us to the sea, the sea drives us to the barbarians; between these two means of death we are either killed or drowned."

THE KINGDOM OF THE SCOTS

These new overlords did not survive in the region for more than 200 years and since no writings of the Picts have come down to us, little is known of this era. However, early in the 7th century, Lothian was infiltrated by Anglians and became part of the Kingdom of Northumbria. 400 years later, this part of the kingdom was given, as a bribe, to Malcolm II (1005–1034) by Earl Adulph of Northumbria in order to dissuade the Scottish monarch from invading Northumbria to avenge an earlier defeat at the hands of Adulph's brother. Malcolm II received the gift gracefully, waited for 12 years, and then defeated Adulph at the battle of Carham.

The consequences of Carham and the Scottish victory were significant and far-reaching. A peace treaty with King Canute was signed, although it is unclear whether or not the English King tried to make Malcolm his liege. The second consequence was more profound. It meant that, for the first time, Scotland was united under a single monarch. From the 11th century, Gaelic became a widely spoken tongue in Lothian, and until Alexander had the misfortune to kill himself by falling off his horse at Kinghorn in 1286, Lothian enjoyed a period of comparative peace.

Although Scotland was now united under a single crown, Lothian paradoxically moved further from the Gaelic–Celtic influence of the North as the monarchical interest identified itself more and more with the Teutonic–English South. Malcolm III, great-grandson of the victor of Carham, married the English princess Margaret, later Saint Margaret, who introduced English customs into the Church and Government. This influence greatly extended itself under the reign of her son David I (1124–1153). Having spent several years at the court of the English King, David returned with Anglo-Norman knights in train to whom he awarded large grants of land. These knights begat the Balliols, Bruces and Comyns who were to play such bloody and romantic roles for the adoptive land of their forbears.

Meanwhile, David's knights owed a double allegiance to the kings of Scotland and England on behalf of land held in both countries. From this time Scotland became a feudal state and, to that extent, a European country.

It may be seen, therefore, that Lothian, in miniature, played its part towards Scotland, as Scotland played towards Europe—that of small state beginning to identify its interests with that of the feudal system in Europe. It required the Wars of Independence before Scotland really saw herself as a separate unity from the territorial presumptions of the Norman–English rulers.

Having, as it were, placed Lothian, not to say Scotland, on the map, the rest of this history will refer almost exclusively to Lothian. Instead of running chronologically through a tedious list of dates, that history will be expressed in what still remains to be seen of the past.

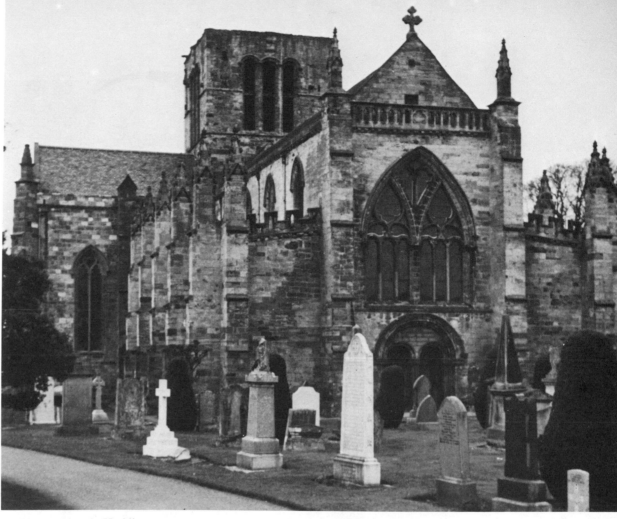

St. Mary's Church, Haddington

HADDINGTON

Haddington first makes its appearance as a burgh in David I's charter of confirmation to Dunfermline Abbey. Alexander II, son of William the Lion, was born here in 1198. Although the name "Haddington" is thought to come from one Haden, a Saxon settler whose hamlet it was origin-

ally, it has also been conjectured that the name derives from Hadina, daughter of the Earl of Surrey and Warren. She was given to Prince Henry, son of David I, in marriage in 1139, and Haddington was her dowry.

As is usual with towns near the English border, there is a long history of sacking and burning, pillage and rape attached to

the town. The most notable of these disasters occurred in 1216 under King John and later, in 1356 under Edward III. Haddington was also the scene of the longest siege in Scottish history when, during the winter of 1548–9, an English garrison defended the town against a Franco-Scottish army. Remains of medieval Haddington include the 12th century

Haddington Town House

church of Saint Martin and the late 14th century church of Saint Mary (Lucerna Laudoniae).

Haddington is a town of bridges and the oldest is the Nungate, dating from the 16th century; it is also one of the oldest in Scotland. The Waterloo Bridge, built in

JOHN KNOX

1817 and the Stevenson Bridge of the later 19th century provide further evidence of native civil engineering skill, pitting its wits against the Tyne.

There exists here too a certain literary and intellectual heritage: Duns Scotus, the medieval philosopher, taught in the town and John Knox *may* have been born in the Gifford Gates. The library of the scholar-linguist John Gray (b. 1646) is now housed in the public library in Newton Port and is a jewel amongst 16th and 17th century collections in Scotland. Some of its treasures include first editions of the "sermons" of John Donne and Bunyan's "Pilgrim's Progress". Jane Welsh, daughter of the town's physician married her tutor Thomas Carlyle, and Robert Burns' mother spent her latter years on Grants' Braes.

The 18th century town of Haddington has been rescued from its apparent fate as a dreary hamlet, and the former splendid architecture has been restored, to be enjoyed by all visitors. The work of the Civic Trust in 1962 was responsible for the rehabilitation of the High Street where all unnecessary signs and overhead wires were scrapped. The street houses, several very fine, have been painted in whites,

blues and ochres to give an overall effect of architectural unity.

The main architectural feature of the town, then, is Town House, partly designed by Robert Adam. Haddington House, the oldest domestic building of the town dating from the 17th century, and Saint Anne's Court (early 18th), are both fine examples of Scottish domestic architecture. Perhaps the most singular feature of the town is the red "Haddingtonshire" stone which is still to be seen in some of the buildings in Church Street. In a spirit of preservation, East Lothian County Council had Mitchell's Close redeveloped and transformed into flats.

Thus this charming town stands not only as a monument to the builders' good taste, but also to the people of the town who refused to live in drabness. And so, once again, in the words of an anonymous versifier of the nineteenth century,

"The famous town of Haddington
 long prosper it will,
 It stands so delightful upon
 the skid hill".

OLD NUNGATE BRIDGE

LINLITHGOW

The name Linlithgow is probably derived from the Brythonic "Linliden" meaning "dear broad lake". The town begins to be of historical importance at the time when Edward I, during the winter of 1301–2, made Linlithgow a platform for his invasion of the North.

Today, the palace dominates the town; Edward began to build onto an existing peel, but Robert the Bruce, after the battle of Bannockburn in 1314, caused it to be destroyed, presumably so that it should never again shield the forces of an English king. Nevertheless, it appears to have been reconstructed by 1334, the year in which Edward Balliol presented the constabu-lary, town and castle of Linlithgow to the English king.

The remains of the palace date from the 15th century. A favourite hobby of the Stewart dynasty, its building was inaugura-ted by James I and completed by James V. One wall of the courtyard was rebuilt by James VI. It became customary, amongst these Stewarts, to settle the palace upon their brides, and so it came to pass that Mary Queen of Scots was born there. Other notable events have occurred of a less charming nature. On the 20th January 1569 James Stewart, Earl of Moray, Regent of Scotland and bastard half-brother to Queen Mary, was travelling from Stirling to Edinburgh. As he passed through Linlithgow, Hamilton of Both-

wellhaugh, a victim of the Regent's high-handed proprietorial ways, shot at him with a hackbut. The wound proved fatal, and a plaque, designed by Sir Noel Paton, the Scottish pre-Raphaelite, com-memorates the assassination.

Many fortunate and many ill-fated figures have slept in Linlithgow Palace. After James VI and I's departure to take up his duties in London, it remained under the auspices of its keepers, the Earls of Linlithgow, and the hall was sometimes used for meetings of the Scots Parliament. Charles I passed one night here in July 1633. Cromwell's revolutionary soldiers garrisoned it from 1651 until 1659 and General Hawley managed, through an ill-conceived attempt to heat the palace, to burn the roof out after his defeat at the hands of Bonnie Prince Charlie at Falkirk in 1746.

In the town itself stands the Cross Well, built in the year 1535. It was too ornate, however, for Cromwell's soldiers who decided that it would look less godless in little pieces. Just to the south of the Palace stands the church of Saint Michael, patron saint of the town. It is very old. A church to the glory of Saint Michael stood on the same site in the reign of David I (1124–1153). A gothic building was erected by Bishop David de Kernham in the reign of Alexander II, but was de-

JAMES V

stroyed by fire in 1424. The present structure was built in the time of James III. Like Saint Giles Cathedral in Edinburgh it has an open work crown tower, though the crown on Saint Michael's is a plain modern structure of gilded metal. The "Blessed Mary" bell in the tower rang the knell for Scotland after the battle at Flodden Field in 1513.

DUNBAR

Dunbar has a very old recorded history. Saint Wilfrid, Bishop of York, was imprisoned in 678 by Ecgfrid and reputedly burnt at the stake at the grand old age of 171! Malcolm Canmore ("Bighead") yielded the town in 1076 to Gospatrick, ex-Earl of Northumbria. Dunbar Castle was inhabited by the Earls of Dunbar and March.

On March 11th 1286, True Thomas of Ercildoune made his prophesy to Patrick, the seventh Earl. The next day Alexander III was killed. This prophecy had a very close bearing on the family of the seventh Earl. His son "Blackbeard", one of the 10 claimants to the throne, was defeated by Wallace in 1296 at Innerwick. This particular family seemed to favour their chances with the English, for the ninth

Dunbar Castle

Dunbar Town House

Earl received Edward II at Dunbar, fleeing from his defeat at Bannockburn in 1314.

However, in 1337, the Earl was away in the North, and the defence of the castle, lately rebuilt, was left to the countess—called "Black Agnes". She seems to have been of a more patriotic disposition than the family she had married into, and for five months she kept at bay the English, headed by the Earls of Arundel and Salisbury. She appears to have delighted in rebuffing her besiegers with insulting rhymes and after Salisbury was humiliated by her gift of white bread and wine, he withdrew.

Black Agnes's brother, the Earl of Moray, died in battle in 1346 and from him her husband, the Earl of Dunbar and March, acquired the title and estates of Moray, thus making him one of the most powerful nobles in Scotland. However, the eleventh Earl was stripped of his possessions by James I after his return to Scotland and James II bestowed the Earldom on his second son.

In 1544, Hertford burnt the town. Queen Mary, however, found herself

Dunbar Harbour

journeying to Dunbar Castle after Rizzio's murder and because she was angered at Darnley's complicity over the affair, she awarded the Captaincy of Dunbar to the Earl of Bothwell. And so, ten weeks after the Kirk o' Field murder of Lord Darnley, Bothwell brought the Queen back to Dunbar where they remained for ten days. The last time Mary visited Dunbar was the night before the battle of Carberry Hill (1567).

Oliver Cromwell, in the only battle up to that time in which he did not have numerical superiority, routed the Scots army at Dunbar on 3rd September 1650; "The Lord of Hosts" against "The Covenant".

Dunbar was twice visited by privateers. In 1779 Paul Jones' ships lay off the town, but they did no damage, and in 1781 Captain Fall threatened the town but did not follow up his words when he saw that preparations were being made for resistance.

Architecturally, the 17th century Town House has an interesting hexagonal tower and beside it stand the remains of the town's Mercat Cross.

Black Agnes

Andrew Lamb's House, Leith

MARY of GUISE

The following year Mary of Guise turned Leith into a fortified town, and ten years later these fortifications successfully withstood the siege of the Protestant Lords until the spring of 1560.

In 1561, Mary Queen of Scots arrived in Leith: this is the town's first important arrival. George IV came by Leith in 1822 and Queen Victoria in 1842.

Although the original single quay has grown into a system of docks, the harbour is what most obviously links Leith with the past. Leith Links still survive where Scotland's kings once golfed. The most interesting building to survive in Leith is Andrew Lamb's house in the Water Close: a sixteenth century town house of the type inhabited by the richer merchants before they moved "up the hill".

GEORGE IV

LEITH

Historically, the connection between Leith and Edinburgh was commercial rather than civic. It has a long history of burnings. In 1313 and 1410 the English set fire to the ships in Leith harbour. In 1544 the Earl of Hertford made the port the starting ground for his expedition through Lothian and the Borders. He retreated, leaving the town in flames. As Protector Somerset, in 1547, he repeated this exercise and in addition captured thirty-five ships.

The Forth Bridges from South Queensferry

SOUTH QUEENSFERRY

South Queensferry is so named on account of Margaret, wife of Malcolm Canmore, having used it as a port from which she crossed between Dunfermline and Edinburgh at the end of the 11th century. Malcolm IV granted to the monks of Dunfermline the right to operate a ferry and in 1641, Charles I raised the town to a Royal Burgh.

HAWES INN

SIR WALTER SCOTT

South Queensferry is important historically as a port of arrival and departure. The Carmelite Priory, built by Sir George Dundas in 1547, was dissolved in 1564. It fell into ruin, but in 1890 was bought by the Scottish Episcopal Church and restored as a mission station. Black Castle, built in 1626, and Plewlands, built within the same decade, are interesting buildings.

The town has two famous literary associations to its credit: under the girders of the Forth Railway Bridge squats the Hawes Inn. Built in 1683, Sir Walter Scott dined Jonathan Oldbuck and Lovell there, and Robert Louis Stevenson made it the scene of the kidnap plot hatched between Captain Hoseason and Ebenezer Balfour. Stevenson is said to have begun to write the novel in Room 13.

15

Hopetoun House

CHAPTER 2

BUILDINGS
AND THEIR HISTORY

Quite simply one of the most splendid houses in the British Isles, Hopetoun is also the best preserved of the Scottish mansions in the grand style. The Hopes of Hopetoun, who became the Earls of Hopetoun and subsequently Marquisses of Linlithgow, built the house, begun in 1699, near Queensferry during the minority of Charles, First Earl of Hopetoun. Sir William Bruce was engaged to build the house, and by 1703 the west facade, small rooms, and staircase of the centre block were completed. In 1721 William Adam enlarged the centre block and added colonnades and pavilions. The east facade is entirely his work.

In 1748, after William's death, his two sons Robert and John continued the work of enlargement, inaugurated by their father. In the main part, their contribu-

tion can be seen in the remodelling of the pavilions and main entrance and, in addition, the interior decoration of the main apartments between 1750 and 1756.

The gardens are laid out in strict symmetry, affording a balance of peculiar charm to the eye. The view from the porch across the lawn and round pond reveals three avenues between the trees. Those to the centre and south-west open onto views of the Deer Park containing the fragments of Stanleyhill Tower, a 17th century house. To the north-west is a vista of Blackness Castle. North of the park is the Bastion Walk, below which is the small Deer Park and its herd of Red Deer.

The main staircase is one of the chief features of the interior of the Bruce house. The stair is of stone and the wood panels heavily carved by Alexander Eizat.

ROBERT ADAM

The Binns

The yellow Drawing Room is a creation of "the genius" Robert Adam. The ceiling is exquisite. Partly gilt spandrels in each corner, and the feature in the centre picked out in gold are of especial interest. The walls are covered in yellow silk brocade made in 1850 and the furniture was created specially for the house by James Cullen, a rival of Chippendale's. Sir Henry Raeburn was knighted in this room by George IV and the finest of the picture collection at Hopetoun are to be found here; amongst others are "The Adoration of the Shepherds" by the studio of Rubens, a composition showing the Emperor Charles V about to depart on a hunting expedition, and "The Grand Canal, Venice" by Canaletto.

THE BINNS

The Binns which now belongs to the National Trust for Scotland was built in 1623 by Thomas Dalyell (pronounced Dee-ell) and in 1820 it received the complete form which is its present aspect. In all, the style is a mixture of Scottish Baronial with Domestic Gothic. The west front is particularly charming and recalls perhaps rather an English house of the first half of the 16th century. Whereas the north front is three storeys in height, the south front is low, having merely one, with an inner court in front.

General Thomas Dalyell is the most famous man to be associated with the house. He carries with his memory, also, a certain notoriety connected with the fact that, being a fanatical Royalist and therefore excluded by Cromwell from the Act of Grace, he sought service with the Czar of Russia from whom, it is said, he learnt to roast prisoners and, in particular, those Covenanters who were unfortunate enough to be apprehended by him.

LIEUT: GENERAL DALZIEL

HAWTHORNDEN

Hawthornden is known to readers of Drummond, the late 16th and early 17th century Scottish poet, as the house of his father and where he, too, spent his life. The River Esk flows through the grounds, and Sir Walter Scott's "wondrous blaze" in "Rosabel" was spied.

"... from Dryden's groves of oak and seen from cavern'd Hawthornden".

There is an old keep with a later house built on to it. The old stronghold is 15th century, although the foundations go back beyond that. It is uncertain whether the poet or his father, or the Douglases from whom the Drummonds bought the grounds and old keep, built the actual house. But it is certain that the old castle was destroyed by the English invasions of 1544 and 1547.

Among the relics at Hawthornden is a 5'2" two-handed sword which belonged to Robert the Bruce. It is said that Queen Mary, that peripatetic monarch, spent three nights here, but tradition has, as yet, been unable to furnish dates.

WILLIAM DRUMMOND

HAWTHORNDEN

BORTHWICK
CASTLE

BORTHWICK CASTLE

Borthwick Castle near Gorebridge is one of the finest of its kind in Scotland. What is particularly impressive is that, although building started in 1430, it stands in practically its original form. It is positioned on the summit of a knoll, known anciently as "The Mote Lockerwort". The castle itself is approached by the west and the gate in the wall surrounding the edifice is defended by a strong bastion tower in the corner. The north and south wings, projecting on this side from the main block, leave a deep, narrow cleft running from parapet to foundation.

On the east side is evidence of the brief cannonade to which the castle was subjected by Cromwell.

The main hall is considered, on account of its great height and beautifully arched roof, to be the finest and most elegantly proportioned of all such halls in Scotland.

A bizarre episode, mentioned in the "New Statistical Account of Scotland" on the authority of Sir Walter Scott, recounts that, in 1547, a Macer of the Archdiocesan Court was despatched to inform Lord Borthwick of his excommunication. Since it was at the time of the Carnival of the "Abbot of Unreason", the festive crowd proceeded to duck the

The local lairds, who had their town houses in Haddington, were in the habit of dining together. Lord Blantyre was a frequent guest of this society but, since he owned no land in the county, his presence caused the Duke some irritation. In order to alleviate this feeling of annoyance at having to suffer Blantyre at the same table, His Grace would amuse himself by offering to sell him Lethington, knowing full well that Blantyre was impecunious.

Now Lord Blantyre had a beautiful cousin, Frances Teresa Stuart, married to the Duke of Lennox and Richmond. She was so lovely—she is said to be the original for "Britannia" on our old pennies—that, naturally, she was a favourite of King Charles. The Duchess, therefore, advised Blantyre to accept the Duke's offer the

next time he should make it. He did offer: Lord Blantyre accepted, and the casket which was sent from the Duchess with the purchasing price remains at Lennoxlove to this day.

Another tale which surrounds Lething-

unfortunate Macer in the duck pond. As it was Christmas time the ducking must have been unpleasant. This, however, was not the end of the poor man's humiliation. The Macer, William Langlands, was then taken into the church where he was persuaded to eat his own writ, torn up and scattered in a bowl of wine to make the meal more digestible. He was then packed off to his masters.

Another incident, relating to Borthwick Castle, is that in the summer of 1567, Queen Mary and the Earl of Bothwell were at the castle when it was surrounded by the barons searching for her. Bothwell departed smartly, leaving Mary to follow suit at night, dressed as a man. Unfortunately, she lost her way on the moor and ended up at Cakemuir Castle. The Battle of Carberry followed.

LENNOXLOVE

In the days of Charles II, Lennoxlove (or Lethington Tower as it then was) belonged to the only Duke of Lauderdale.

LENNOXLOVE

ton and the Duke of Lauderdale concerns the wall surrounding the demesne. Apparently when James, Duke of York, came to Scotland in 1680, he remarked to the Duke that he believed there to be not one walled park in Scotland. Whereupon the wall was built and is believed to have been, indeed, the first residential park in Scotland, enclosed by such a wall.

The Old Tower of the house is certainly not later than 1400 and is the most interesting aspect of Lennoxlove. A later tower, built by the Maitlands about 1644 stands at the east end of the south front of the extended house. This tower was raised in height in 1810.

BIEL HOUSE

Standing just three miles from Dunbar, Biel still displays the original 14th century walls of the "fortalice of Biel". These are incorporated in the massive square tower. The entrance front faces north, and the Gothic Arch, a gateless gateway, stands at right angles to it on the left as the observer faces it. The west portion of the wall of the house is higher than the east, and battlemented.

From the south side, the three sections compounding the house are easily distinguishable. The oldest is in the middle. On this south side three staggered terraces extend from the house to a haugh (or meadow) which, in turn, runs to the Biel Burn. The terraces were originally laid out by the 1st Lord Belhaven, a strong supporter of Charles I. Eventually, Lord Belhaven found himself in Kew, working in disguise as a skilled Scottish gardener, following the final defeat of the king. The second Lord Belhaven, coming as he did of a family of strongly held opinion, marked the Act of Union with an inscription placed in the house which reads

"Traditionis Scotiae Anno Primo, 1707"

—in the first year of the betrayal of Scotland.

BIEL HOUSE

Detail of Staircase,
Yester House

YESTER HOUSE

Finished by William Adam in the year 1745, it is said that the workmen on the roof threw slates at the Dragoons quitting the battlefield of Prestonpans.

The house runs east-west with the architectural facade facing north. The entrance, however, is on the west. The centre piece in the north side is classical with the triumphal arch motif pre-dominating.

Inside, the house is light, the hall is large and handsome and projected back almost the whole length of the house. One of the interesting portraits, of Lord Charles Hay, recalls the story of how, when he commanded the King's Company of Grenadiers at Fontenoy in 1745, the English and French troops were drawn up in line at 50 paces distance. "Gentlemen of the French, fire first" he cried, to which the Comte d'Auteroche replied "No, sir, we never fire first." Nineteen officers and 380 soldiers of the French guard fell. The drawing-room is very fine and is said to be one of the finest of its size in Scotland.

The old Yester Castle was the "Goblin Hall" of the wizard Sir Hugo de Gifford. He was said to have built it with spirits under his control. There is not very much left of the Castle which lies upwards from

WILLIAM ADAM

22

Malleny House

the modern house along the Hopes Water. A legend says that any member of the Hay family who interferes with the castle is doomed to sudden death. In 1861, when the then Lord Gifford uncovered the stairs which had been buried, the prophecy came true, for Lord Gifford was killed almost immediately afterwards.

MALLENY HOUSE

Malleny, near Balerno, is owned now by the National Trust for Scotland. The proprietors of the house from 1647 until 1882 were the Scotts, who held lands in the rising moorland south-west of Edinburgh, including Malleny itself, Clerkington, Lymphoy, Currie, Harperrig and Buteland. They came originally from Ayrshire and entered the legal profession in the 18th century. There is a group of portraits of the Scott family, including the Alexander Nasmyth picture of John Scott —who added the Regency wing to the house—given by the descendant of the family, Mr. Wrey Gardiner, to the National Trust for Scotland to hang in Malleny in perpetuity.

The plain, rectangular part of the house was built by Sir Thomas Murray of Kilbaberton in 1634, the King's architect in Scotland to Charles I. The garden enclosure and dovecot go back to the 17th century.

PINKIE HOUSE

Dunfermline Abbey, founded in 1072, had, as one of its possessions, Pinkie House, which was originally built about the year 1190. Today it is the main building in Loretto School. The square tower or keep is the oldest remaining part of the modern

PINKIE HOUSE

house and is still its central feature. This is held to have been built in 1390 which points to the probability that it was indeed erected on the site of a smaller tower, built by the monks, in the possession of Dunfermline Abbey. The house itself is in the L shape, a familiar Scottish form, one block facing east and the other facing south and joined at a south-east angle, the interior fronts being therefore west and north. The main entrance is in the west front—the central part being the old tower.

Chancellor Seton built the house, as it stands today, in 1612 and 1613. He built a well-canopy in the centre of what he evidently intended to be his courtyard. There are many different and striking architectural features which blend with the whole—a Jacobean window over the porch; crow stepped gable; battlemented parapet and square tower.

In the house itself is a unique room known as the "Pinkie Gallery" or the "Blue Room". It is 85 feet long and is evidently the work of Italian artists, a rarity in Scottish interior design.

CARBERRY TOWER

Situated in beautifully wooded parkland, the tower faces westward and is covered with climbing plants, giving it a very charming appearance. It is not certain who built the house, but it is thought that an Edinburgh advocate, Hugh Rigg, a man of some considerable influence, may have constructed the tower in 1543 since there is no mention of a dwelling place before this date. The tower, which is an oblong block built for strength, has been added to from time to time giving us the house as it is today.

CARBERRY TOWER

In the grounds of Carberry Tower is Carberry Hill, where Mary Queen of Scots saw the Crown lost to her. The confederate Lords rallying round the dead Darnley met Bothwell's royal army on the hill and, all day, whilst Bothwell stood and issued challenges, the royal army melted away. There is an inscription on the hill which states: "At this spot Mary Queen of Scots, after the escape of Bothwell, mounted her horse and surrendered herself to the Confederate Lords, June 15, 1567". There is also another monolith which has inscribed on its surface: "These entrenchments were thrown up by the English before the battle of Pinkie, September 10, 1547, and afterwards made use of by Queen Mary, June 15, 1567."

CHAPTER 3

THE HEART OF MIDLOTHIAN

It was not until 6000 B.C., a comparatively late date, that the Forth Estuary began to be inhabited by Man. These people comprised hunters and fishers, and they remained living in this fashion off shellfish, and what they could catch on the land until 3000 B.C., when the first farmers to come to Scotland from the continent coasted up the western and eastern searoutes.

With the farmers came the knowledge of metal-working in copper, bronze and gold: with this knowledge came the need for trade. By 1500 B.C., the British Isles were part of a European trading pattern, and the burials of these traders and farmers within the Edinburgh area reveal an increased concentration of population in this region.

From the 8th century B.C. the continental trading in bronze metal-work was intensified, and the finds of tools and weapons of this period, made in bronze, suggest that there may have been a port somewhere on the Water of Leith in the Stockbridge–Dean Village area. The next archaeological evidence which we have dates from some apparent threat which caused little hilltop forts to be built; this threat possibly consisted in the first Roman advance into this part of the country.

Literary rather than archaeological sources became the main point of study for the origins of Edinburgh after the Romans had departed. The first mention of Edinburgh is as Duneidin; the fort of Eidin, in a narrative poem of the 6th century A.D. known as the Gododdin.

As we have seen already, the Northumbrian kingdom, which stretched from Deira (modern Yorkshire) upwards through Bernicia (Durham, Northumberland, Berwickshire), must have made of ancient Edinburgh, or Duneidin, a frontier fort. But with Malcolm II's victory at Carham, the Scottish border moved south.

THE CASTLE

Edinburgh is unusual as a great city, for it is an urban commonplace for such a capital to straddle a river. Edinburgh's river is the Water of Leith; hardly the Tiber, Euphrates, Ganges or Seine. She grew, instead, in the Scottish manner, out of a single street and in high and draughty exposure.

St. Margaret's Chapel is the oldest building in Edinburgh. It grows out of the castle rock, created there by the niece of Edward the Confessor, Queen, fugitive from the Normans, and saint. 1090 therefore becomes a real date for us; history henceforth becomes tolerably well chronicled. Malcolm Canmore and Margaret did not establish Edinburgh as their capital, which remained across the Forth at Dunfermline. It was their son, David I, who achieved this.

The original masonry of the Chapel is Norman, dressed rectangular blocks of freestone. Inside is a semi-circular stone-vaulted apse and there are alterations, such as the vault of the nave of 150 years ago; but the whole, a box of stone, remains of Queen Margaret's time. It has a holy aura that withstood all the sieges to which the castle itself was subjected.

This is the first building of what may loosely be termed "Edinburgh as we know it". It is interesting that Queen Margaret, brought up in Hungary, was the first person to bring Scotland truly within the orbit of Europe. Queen Margaret suppressed the old Celtic church, and brought in representatives of the new integrated monastery orders both to run the Church and to provide a Civil Service for the feudal monarchy.

Across the Palace Yard—The Close—from the 1914–19 National War Memorial,

designed by Sir Robert Lorimer, is the Great Hall, built by James IV. Its interior style, particularly the carved masks of men and beasts by the end of the hammer-beams and the carved stone supporting corbels, is of that Scottish Renaissance character very evocative of James's reign. Underneath the Hall are the Casemates, vaulted chambers used as prisons right up until the Napoleonic wars.

The Palace itself stands to the east side of the Close. As a palace it is not particularly impressive because the Castle as a residence was replaced by the more congenial Palace of Holyrood. However, the castle owes much of its appearance to James VI and I for it was heightened in honour of a return visit he made to Scotland in 1617. The room in which Mary Queen of Scots bore Darnley's son, the future King of England and Scotland, is relatively intact.

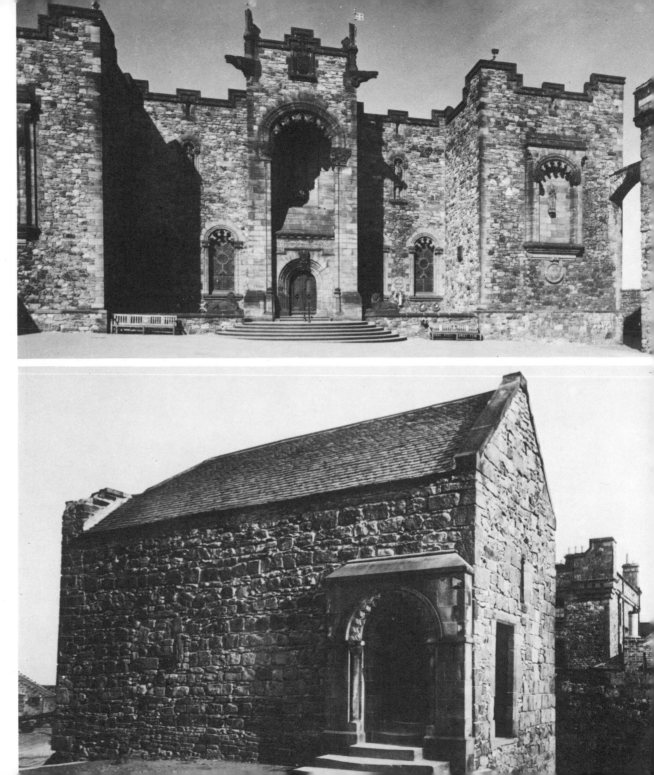

Above: National War Memorial: Detail of bas-relief "The Tunnellers' Friends"

Right: National War Memorial, Edinburgh Castle
Below right: St. Margaret's Chapel

There is much history which attaches itself to the Castle. The most remarkable narrative is the story of the Honours of Scotland. The Honours, which can be seen in the Crown Room, consist of the Crown, Sceptre and Sword of State. This particular crown was remodelled for James V in 1540, its original is unknown. Diamonds, pearls, topazes, amethysts and carbuncles are the jewels, and the coronet is garnished with fleur-de-lys and crosses. The Sword of State was a gift from Julius II, made in 1507 and the sceptre was also a papal gift, sent in 1494 by Alexander VI to James IV. The latter was remodelled, like the crown, by his son.

Charles I wanted the Honours to be sent to England for his Coronation, but instead had to come to Holyrood to be crowned King of Scotland. During the English Revolution, the Honours were hidden in Dalkeith but were surrendered

The Honours of Scotland

and the Honours were discovered in the great oak chest. Sir Walter Scott was one of the witnesses present.

As a whole, the architecture of the Castle hardly commends itself to the aesthete. Rather its greatness—its architecture comprising a medley of buildings good, bad and indifferent—resides in its history and its symbolic associations. It was a Castle that was hardly lived in, and yet it represents the beginning of a consciousness of belonging to something larger and even more ancient than Scotland itself—a beginning which was guided by Saint Margaret.

Visitors often ask, "was the castle impregnable?" Actually it was twice taken, once by Bruce's nephew, Randolph, during the Wars of Independence, and once in 1572 when the supporters of the Regent Morton starved out its defendants, the supporters of Queen Mary, and eventually forced their surrender by poisoning the well at source.

when the castle was given up to the Presbyterians in 1640. Thereafter they were taken to Dunnottar Castle, on its rock on the Kincardine coast, and smuggled out of that Castle whilst it was being besieged by the "Oliverians", by Christian Fletcher, the wife of James Granger, minister of Kinneff. The minister buried them under the floor of the kirk until they were triumphantly restored to Edinburgh Castle in May 1662. In 1707,

after the Act of Union, there was a great deal of worry in case the Honours were to go south after all. It was therefore necessary to include a special clause in the Act by which they "are never more to be used, but kept constantly in the castle in Edinburgh". They were locked away and forgotten. However a suspicion that they had, in fact, been taken south was only alleviated when, with the permission of George IV, the Crown Room was opened

HOLYROOD

For long, Edinburgh was confined to the ridge running from the Castle to the Abbey at Holyrood. Legend has it that Queen Margaret's son, David I, broke a holy day by hunting and was saved from death on the antlers of a stag. As a result he built the abbey in penance. An antlered stag, with the cross on its forehead, is the Coat of Arms of the Burgh of the Canongate, and Queen Margaret's cross of

The Arms of the Burgh of Canongate

ebony and silver gave its name to Holyrood.

Today the Palace dwarfs the church and it is very difficult to tell what Holyrood Abbey actually was. Only the roofless nave of the Abbey-Church still stands, a monument to the neglect that befell many churches after the Reformation in Scotland. Needless to say, during Hertford's plundering of the abbeys in the south of Scotland, the church suffered some depredation, notably in the removal of the brass lectern which still resides in the church at St. Albans. Still more, in granting the sinecure of Holyrood to his seven-year-old bastard son Robert Stewart, James V ensured the fate of the Abbey. This Commendator of Holyrood used some of the stones of the Abbey to build himself a

MARY, QUEEN of SCOTS

house right in front of the west entrance. In 1569, he exchanged for the bishopric of Orkney the abbacy and perquisites of Holyrood with Adam Bothwell. This gentleman was impious, and mean to boot; under his ministrations the Abbey-Church fell into worse sorts. He conducted the nuptials forced upon Mary Queen of

Holyrood Palace

BOTHWELL

Scots by the Earl of Bothwell and yet was the Queen's harshest accuser at Northampton. These nuptials were particularly grim since they took place according to the Protestant rite—which showed how much Mary had lost her grip—and lines from Ovid's Fifth Book of Fasti "Mense malas maius nubere vulgus est" were paraphrased as "Wantons marry in the month of May", a sign of the deep rooted Scots prejudice against May marriages; witness the old saying: "Marry in May and regret it for ay".

The next piece of hooliganism followed in 1567 when the Earl of Glencairn, following the imprisonment of Mary, smashed all the statues and altars. The Commendator had previously avoided responsibility for reparation of damage by cutting off the choir and transepts, reducing the church to its present form. However, for James VI and I the truncated nave must have been under tolerable repair since he chose to marry his betrothed, Anne of Denmark, here, and it was somehow patched up for Charles I's coronation. Charles II eventually ordered that the remains of the choir and cross kirk be demolished so that they might not clutter up his palace.

The Abbey-Church had one last burst of glory, when James VII and II converted it into a Chapel Royal with an altar and stalls for his revived Knights of the

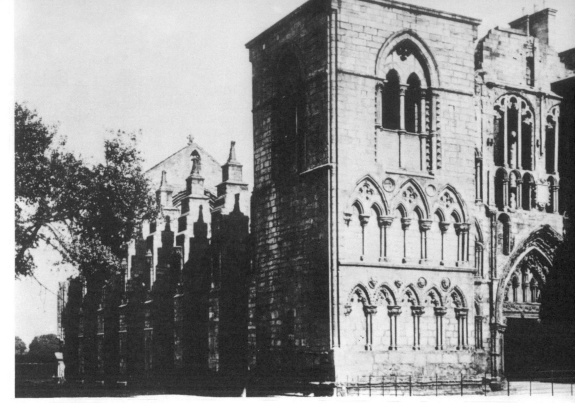

The ruin of Holyrood Abbey

Thistle. The last glory of the church was destroyed by the mob on hearing that the Prince of Orange had arrived in London; the Royal vault was broken into and the coffins smashed.

Long before the building of the Palace, the Kings of Scotland were constant visitors to the Abbey. Between 1178, when the Augustinians first took up residence here, and Hertford's depredations, the Abbey-Church was at the height of sacred (and profane) splendour. The abbey gardens were cultivated and planted with vegetables, fruit and flowers; garlic, strawberries and primroses. But the garden of earthly delight took its toll upon the

rarified and spiritual atmosphere; after a shameful brawl between the canons and some sailors at Leith, the Pope decided to take matters in hand. In 1450 he appointed his own man, abbot Archibald Crawford. The new abbot built the flying buttresses which still support the wall of the church. His successor, Bellenden, most probably built the Chapel of St. Antony, whose ruins stand on the Salisbury Crags behind the Abbey. It was also during his abbacy that the Holyrood Ordinale was written, a fine parchment folio. A Crichton followed, who was the last soundly spiritual soul. Nepotism wreaked havoc soon after this.

The main front of the Palace of Holyroodhouse is the work of Sir William Bruce, effected during the reign of Charles II. The entry is flanked by two tower blocks, each capped with twin turrets, but this symmetry is misleading for whilst the northern one is the James IV tower of 1500, its opposite is again the work of Bruce. Indeed, Charles II conceived a great affection for this home of the Stewarts, surprisingly however, since he never set foot in it. He commanded, as we have seen, Scotland's greatest living architect, Sir William Bruce, to take charge of its completion. The King inspected all the plans himself and made modifications to them.

From 1679 until 1682, James, Duke of York was resident in Holyrood as Commissioner, the last time that royalty has been resident in Scotland in any official capacity.

One of the most infamous exploits in the history of Scotland took place in this Palace. There are various accounts of it, several conflicting, but the facts of the incident are as follows: on Saturday, 9 March 1566 a supper party given by Queen Mary was in progress; it was interrupted

LORD DARNLEY

by the curious apparition of Darnley on the Privy staircase, followed by the even more curious sight of Patrick, Lord Ruthven, complete with steel cap and armour, bright eyed from the fever which would shortly consume him. In the ensuing confusion, Andrew Ker of Fawdonside, Patrick Bellenden, George Douglas, Thomas Scott and Henry Yair rushed into the room towards the Queen's secretary, Rizzio. He was plucked from the Queen's skirts and butchered in the next room.

What is certain is that Darnley, Mary's husband, felt Rizzio to be responsible for the decline of his influence and his vanity made him painfully aware of this. It may also be that Mary thought her weak and vicious husband had intended to encompass her own destruction, and incidentally, that of her unborn child—the future James VI—in this assault on her secretary.

One curious aspect of Holyroodhouse was its retention of its right of sanctuary held, presumably, since the days of the Canons. Of course the hereditary keepers, the Dukes of Hamilton, kept rooms there, but in the 18th and 19th centuries, the place was a warren of little flats inhabited by debtors. There have been several very famous of these so-called "Abbey Lairds".

In 1796, the future Charles X of France became an "Abbey Laird" because, as an exile from the French Revolution, he was probably in debt. It can be said that he lived as befits a king in the Palace. One of Edinburgh's Lord Provosts has been known to take up accommodation within these precincts, and Thomas de Quincy, getting into debt with the Holyrood landlady herself, had to find sanctuary from his sanctuary. An 1880 Act rendered the right of sanctuary superfluous.

THE CITY IN THE MIDDLE AGES

Roman civilization by-passed Edinburgh altogether: the nearest the Romans came were to Cramond and Inveresk, and later to Duddingston and Dunsappie Hill.

When David I transferred the seat of government to Edinburgh, the whole summit of the Castle rock was enclosed, and a civilian suburb began to wend its way down the narrow street of Castle Hill to fan out at the head of the West Bow. The West Bow led to the Grassmarket and between the houses ran closes and wynds down to two back roads, one of which, the old cattle road—the Cowgate—remains to this day. The houses themselves were of the wood-framed type with plaster or clay infilling, much like their English and Continental counterparts. Edward I, "the hammer of the Scots", left none standing after he burnt the town. Edinburgh

EDINBURGH

FROM A MAP OF 1573

TO LEITH

CALTON HILL

CASTLE

NOR' LOCH

emerges in some shape after James II built the King's Wall in 1450.

The character of the city is no longer that of an open, prosperous and peaceful one: it is now constricted and space is at a premium. However, after Flodden and the death of James IV in 1513, another wall was built to protect an area lying well south of the Cowgate and this enlarged the city. The Flodden Wall ran south from the south-east corner of the Castle rock, across the end of the Grassmarket, bulged out to enclose Greyfriars Church, ran above Candlemaker Row, by the Kirk o' Field and turned north short of the Pleasance. Finally it followed the border between Edinburgh and Canongate, turned west near to where Waverley Station is today, and ended at the North Loch, which served to defend the city from the north. The Gateways were as follows: West Port at the end of the Grassmarket; Bristo Port; Cowgate Port; and Netherbow Port at the Canongate. This remained the boundary of the city until the development of the New Town in the middle of the 18th century.

ST. GILES

St. Giles' Cathedral probably dominated the High Street by the end of the fifteenth century. The Preston Aisle was erected in 1454 to enshrine the arm bone of St. Giles, and the choir was enlarged in 1462. In 1467 this parish church was elevated to the status of a collegiate

Crown spire of St. Giles

St. Giles High Kirk

church. The lantern spire may have been completed in 1495; this was repaired by John Mylne in 1646 who added the crown.

St. Giles has been unfortunate in its restorers. William Burn managed to re-face the Cathedral with paving stones in 1829, although Chambers tried to repair the damage with his alteration between 1872 and 1893. Sir Robert Lorimer designed the Thistle Chapel in St. Giles in 1911 which is really too ornate for the original Norman stonework of the Cathedral.

Mass was sung in St. Giles for the last time in 1560, and in 1573, realizing that the interior was too large for the new low-church habits of the reformers, the earliest of these reformers split St. Giles into four chapels. However, under Charles I, St. Giles became a cathedral between 1633 and 1638, and in 1637, since the Episcopacy was not popular, the famous incident relating to Jenny Geddes and her stool occurred.

After the signing of the Solemn League and Covenant of 1643 in the Preston Aisle—since called the Assembly Aisle— St. Giles was used, in the normal way, as arsenal, prison, and unofficial poorhouse, although this last might possibly be con-sidered a more proper use of a church than at first one might imagine.

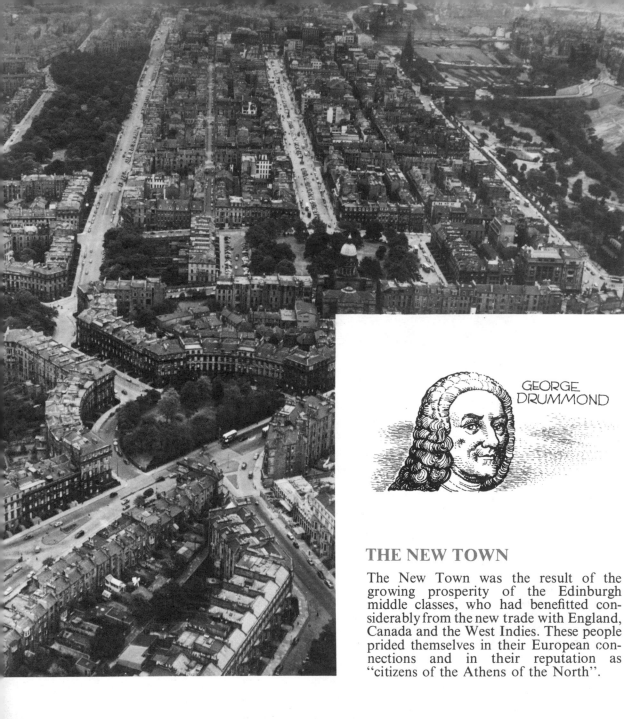

In 1752 a pamphlet was published in Edinburgh entitled "Proposals for carrying on certain Public Works in the City of Edinburgh". This call to action combined economic with vaguely patriotic motives: the arts of wealth and the arts of peace were both to be given full expression. But what is remarkable about these proposals is that they were actually carried out during the course of the next 80 years. George Drummond, considered by some to have been the most influential person in Edinburgh during the 18th century, was elected Lord Provost at various intervals from 1725 until 1764. In 1738, under his auspices, a new Infirmary·was begun—in what is now Infirmary Street—under Royal Charter. After having done so much to establish this building, Drummond entered with zeal into the "Proposals" of 1752.

The Exchange may be said to be the first building of the New Town, begun in 1753, but it was never used for the purpose it was intended to fulfil; the Edinburgh merchants continued to deal in the streets.

GEORGE DRUMMOND

THE NEW TOWN

The New Town was the result of the growing prosperity of the Edinburgh middle classes, who had benefitted considerably from the new trade with England, Canada and the West Indies. These people prided themselves in their European connections and in their reputation as "citizens of the Athens of the North".

Charlotte Square, North Side

This building stands in the High Street and it was not long before a way of improving the Eastern Road, which ran from the Old Town round the east side of Calton Hill, was entertained. The idea, of course, put forward in the proposals, was to make as much use as possible of the land on the other side of the North Loch or Nor' Loch as it was called at the time.

Drainage of the Nor' Loch—as put forward in the "Proposals"—began in 1759, and in 1763 an advertisement inviting tenders for a bridge to be built across it was published. After many setbacks, including an initial collapse, the bridge was completed for use in 1772. The next important project was the proposed building of Register House. To be built "In the area at the end of the New Bridge" Robert and James Adam drew up an elevation of the building in 1772. On 27 June 1774, the foundation stone was laid. It was

finished, again after many difficulties, by the beginning of the Napoleonic Wars. One of these difficulties included a 6 year period of rooflessness as "the most magnificent pigeon-house in Europe". The bridging of the Cowgate followed: the New North Bridge connected the city to the lands of the north, and what was now needed was a similar connection with the south. After all, the first truly modern building project—and the first true square —that Edinburgh ever had was being built in the 1760s: George Square. This was, it must be pointed out, not part of the proposed New Town, as it lay outwith the Royalty which was to develop the lands to the north. Still, it was, by 1770, the most fashionable area of Edinburgh; it must needs be linked to the city.

By July 1767, it was clear that James Craig's plan was going to be adopted by the Lord Provost with regard to the build-

ing in "the fields to the north". His plan was particularly sensible and orthodox: it was mechanical and symmetrical, making use of the idea of "linked squares" used by Héré de Corny in the "New Town" of Nancy in France, but without the freedom and elegance employed by the Frenchman. So far as we know, Craig was not invited to design any of the buildings that were to form his plan.

Basically, Craig's New Town consists of two squares—Charlotte and St. Andrew's—joined by a central street—George Street—and flanked by two others—Queen Street and Princes Street. The design is hardly original since Cardinal Richelieu ordered almost exactly the same design for the town of Richelieu, near Tours, in 1633. Nor does it overwhelm the observer with its fund of imagination. Why, then, has it been so successful? The answer lies in the use of the site. Princes Street and Queen Street have houses on only one side of the street and this increases and enhances the spaciousness which was so dearly loved by the men of taste of the 18th century.

By 1781, St. Andrew's Square had been entirely built and building was going on as far west as Hanover Street. Charlotte Square proved a slightly more difficult case. The fact was that not all the land between Calton Hill and Queensferry Road belonged to Edinburgh. The Earl of Moray had a servitude over "90 feet in breadth of ground belonging to the community" according to the Lord Provost. However, by 1791, this set-back had been overcome, and Robert Adam was commissioned to produce a frontage scheme for the houses of the square. This was a new move, for up to this date the design for the houses in Princes Street, George Street and Queen Street had been rather unimaginative in design and uniformly plain in execution. The elevations were drawn up by Adam in 1791, and its author died the following year.

Charlotte Square is a rectangle 500 feet by 500 feet, with streets entering at each corner. A garden occupies the whole of the centre of the square. Every side is three storeys high, and the north and south sides are centered on a pediment, mounted on four Corinthian pillars. Balustrades,

festoons and circular panels serve to enrich the appearance of the whole. The north side is the best preserved. It is a marvellous achievement, and was not completed until 30 years after Robert Adam's death.

In May 1785, the South Bridge Act was passed and in August the foundation stone was laid. The new bridge, or viaduct, was driven through the busiest areas of the Old Town; the Trustees paid for the area between Niddry's Wynd and Martine's Wynd, also the area fronting the Cowgate—the former fish market. This was quite a considerable piece of civil engineering. The foundation of the central pier is said to have been dug 22 feet deep and the whole is just over 1,000 feet in length and, although not so high overall as North Bridge, there are no fewer than 19 arches. The Bridge was open by the summer of 1788.

The University, however, was not so

easily accomplished. It was designed by Robert Adam, but the University as it stands at the corner of Chambers' Street and South Bridge is hardly an Adam building. The east front, except the dome, is pure Adam; the elevation inside the courtyard facing the main gate is almost exactly as planned by Adam. The remaining elevations are by Playfair. The foundation stone was laid on 16 November 1789, but with the outbreak of war in February 1793 work stopped completely. Pitt's war budget did not allow of funds in 1800 for it could not find room for expensive public works. Everything was laid aside.

Public building revived about 1806 with the conversion of the old buildings in Parliament Close. Accommodation for the Supreme Courts in Scotland were inadequate and Robert Reid carried out radical alterations between 1807 and 1810. Waterloo Place and Bridge, the eastern approach to Princes Street, were begun in

Adam's drawing for the new South Bridge

The Upper Library, Old College, Edinburgh University

1816 and completed by 1822. The bridge is over a ravine of a height of 50 feet. This opening up of Princes Street to the east implied the building of a whole new part of the town between Edinburgh and Leith —the so-called "Calton Hill Scheme". William Playfair was the architect whose plan was accepted late in 1819. Building began almost at once. The "Calton Hill Scheme" had one serious drawback; it was observed by Playfair that people of fashion were gathering in the western part of the town. Calton Hill was also cut off from Craig's New Town by the intrusion of public buildings such as Register House and the new Post Office in Waterloo Place. Thus the newly planned area lying to the north of London Road—intersecting streets, octagons, circuses and trees —was hardly built according to its visionary author. Calton Hill itself, of course, is now littered with buildings, the left-overs, it seems, of the New Town development. There is Craig's Observatory, an ugly, embattled edifice which is perhaps the only known building attributable to him which still exists. Near to it stands the New Observatory by Playfair in heavy, Roman Doric. Also by Playfair is the monument to Dugald Stewart taking the aspect of a small circular temple, as does the Burns monument by Thomas Hamilton a little further down the hill. The Nelson Monument, taller than these, a curious inverted telescope by Robert Burn, dominates the other buildings.

However, the most poignant and beautiful structure on Calton Hill is the National Monument "the pride and poverty of Scotland" according to Playfair. It was the beginning of a scheme for a memorial to those fallen in the Napoleonic Wars but funds ran out after 16 months of building. It is, albeit incomplete, the loveliest construction on the Hill.

Waterloo Bridge from Calton Road

The National Monument, Calton Hill

WILLIAM PLAYFAIR

There was something left over from the 1780s which at last, 40 years later, had become increasingly burdensom on the minds of the Trustees, prospective architects, builders and men of taste. An Earthen Mound had built up by the 1780s as a result of the excavations in what was now Craig's New Town, and although several schemes had been put forward none had been followed up. As early as 1781, proposals had been announced to construct an early communication from the Lawn-Market to Princes Street and builders were invited to deposit rubbish, from excavations elsewhere, on the west side of Princes Street. This grew into the Mound and in 1806 the Bank of Scotland was completed on the summit. The Royal Institution (now the Royal Scottish Academy) was the next strategically placed public building; completed in 1826 it stands at the north end of the

39

The Royal Scottish Academy

Mound, off Princes Street. It was much improved into the building as it stands today, with side porticos and a double row of columns at its Princess Street entrance. It was also extended southwards by 100 feet.

The building of the Royal Academy at the beginning of the 19th century led to some very complex new developments in the centre of the city. This plan included the use of the Mound as a communication between the High Street and Princes Street, the construction of a road south from the High Street, and the joining of the High Street to the western end of the New Town. An important consideration at this time was the question of the open space south of Princes Street and to the east of the Mound. The Faculty of Advocates took a strong line in 1825 opposing any suggestion that buildings could be introduced into that part of the city, and from that year the future of the Mound was discussed within the constraint that the ground between the Old Town and Princes Street remain an open space. After a great deal of wrangling, it was decided by 1834 to lower the High Street and to reduce the slope of the hill: Bank Street was also lowered and a few improvements made to the roadway on the upper half of the Mound. This was completed in the spring of the following year.

Whilst this was being effected, another Bill was passed in Parliament in 1827: this was to fulfil the need for the communication desired between the Old Town and the western New Town, and that desired stretching from the Old Town towards the south. Building was forbidden on the Meadows or on Bruntsfield Links. Efforts were now concentrated on the building of

The Bank of Scotland building on the Mound

Ainslie Place

two new bridges to facilitate communications—the small King's Bridge for the west approach and the larger "new South Bridge" (called King George IV Bridge today). This latter bridge was in use by the summer of 1834.

Private development of the New Town was a wholly 19th century event: the most westerly point of the New Town at the beginning of the century was Charlotte Square. North and west of the square was open country. This land was owned at the time by the Trustees of Heriot's Hospital, the Earl of Moray, Sir Francis Walker and Henry Raeburn the painter (knighted in the Yellow Drawing Room at Hopetoun by George IV in 1822). Construction, outside the strict confines of the New

Drummond Place

Doorway, Heriot Row. *Opposite:* Ann Street

Town, began in 1799 with the building of Duke Street, Elder Street and York Place. These were completed in 1804. By 1823 Royal Circus (elevation by Playfair), Drummond Place and Great King Street were built; the street parallel to Queen Street, and forming the southern boundary of this, the "second New Town"—Heriot Row—was begun in 1803. Included in this complex are Northumberland Street, Jamaica Street (now a "vacant lot") and Abercromby Place, begun in 1814. India Street was built between 1819 and 1823.

Sir Henry Raeburn began his own private development in 1813 with Raeburn Place and Dean Street; Ann Street (named for his wife) followed, and India Place was begun in 1823. The area west of Princes Street, comprising Shandwick Place, Atholl Crescent and Coates Crescent, was planned as early as 1801 but the approach to the Old Town via Castle Terrace was not open until 1830. The Hospital was again the superior of these lands. Gillespie Graham found his niche designing the last of the post-war Georgian developments of the Earl of Moray's properties—namely Randolph Crescent, Ainslie Place and Moray Place. The design appears to have been conceived as a whole and is at once charming and majestic. It is the architecture of the conqueror.

After 86 years the development was completed. Enormous sums of money had been spent, some of it inevitably wasted; there had been arguments galore and setbacks both architectural and economic. The Napoleonic Wars had also led to delay. None of these have detracted from the very fine achievement which had been inaugurated by the visionaries and planners of 1752.

HENRY RAEBURN

John Cockburn: *Detail from a portrait in the Scottish National Portrait Gallery*

MEN OF LOTHIAN

JOHN COCKBURN of ORMISTON (1679–1758)

John Cockburn has been described as "the father of Scottish agriculture".

He was the eldest son of Adam Cockburn, Lord Justice Clerk for Scotland. As a young man he served in the last Scottish Parliament, and then was M.P. for the county of Haddington (later known as East Lothian) at Westminster from 1707 until 1741.

Despite his long absences in London, John Cockburn managed his father's Lothian estate of Ormiston for 20 years.

before himself succeeding to it in 1734.

In every way he was a great "improver" and became one of the leading figures of the Agricultural Revolution.

Cockburn argued that tenant farmers granted only short leases had no incentive to carry out improvements to their land. Under his management a lease of 38 years was granted to Robert Wight—and this lease could be renewed for 19-year spells indefinitely. Other Ormiston tenants were later to benefit similarly. Realising that both they and their descendants were sure to benefit, these tenants co-operated (more or less willingly) with Cockburn and carried out his suggestions.

The old runrig system (strips of land allocated to various tenants and farmed by all of them as a team) was abandoned at Ormiston, and fields were enclosed to form new farm-units round specially built steadings. The ditches and hedges of Ormiston became famous.

So did the crops grown on this newly enclosed land. Robert Wight grew turnips (then a pioneering crop) in drills, and cultivated them with the plough. Cockburn master-minded this experiment and many others, often at long distance, using letters. He had his own ideas, too, on wheat, grass-seeds, livestock and gardening.

As early as 1724 potatoes (another pioneering crop in Scotland) were growing in Cockburn's garden, and two years later Wight was growing them in open fields, perhaps the first Scot to do so.

The potato was probably introduced to Ormiston by Irish immigrants brought over by Cockburn to instruct his people on how to grow flax, spin yarn and weave linen. (He laid out the second bleach-field in Scotland.)

But Cockburn did not restrict himself to the land in his activities. After 1734 he had the village of Ormiston rebuilt to his own spacious design and high standards. As markets for his barley crops he erected a brewery and a distillery.

In 1736 Cockburn formed a local branch (or club) of the Edinburgh Society of Improvers. Other Lothian landowners joined, including Lord Drommore, the Earl of Stair, the Chief of the Clan Macleod and the Duke of Perth. Cockburn, as chairman, publicised his own improvements and the others were not slow to take note and act accordingly.

Any land unfit for farming at Ormiston was planted with trees. These included silver firs, evergreen oaks, oriental planes and sweet chestnuts. In the garden, wall and espalier fruit trees were put in.

Unfortunately Cockburn was to suffer for his improvements. The long leases did not pay the landlord at that time, he borrowed money (the estate was already pledged for a £10,000 loan) and finally he had to sell the estate, about 1848, to the Earl of Hopetoun. (The club he chaired was wound up in 1847.)

John Cockburn died poor, but he is remembered today as the great pioneering Scottish land-owner of his time, a man of enthusiasm, imagination and driving energy.

PARAFFIN YOUNG

James Young is regarded as the founder of the Scottish Oil Industry. Young came from Glasgow—the Drygate—where his father was a joiner, and his first job was putting the finishing touches to the coffins made by his parent. In the evenings, Young went to the Andersonian Institute in order to relieve himself of the macabre work which he accomplished during the day time, and to continue his education. David Livingstone, the future explorer, attended the same classes as Young.

In the fulfillment of time, Young himself became an assistant lecturer and after working in London as assistant to the Professor of Chemistry at University College, he moved to Manchester as Scientific adviser to Tennant's Chemical Works. Lyon Playfair, a former pupil of Young's at the Andersonian Institute—the parent of Strathclyde University—wrote to him in Manchester reporting the find of a thin black irridescent liquid and sent a sample. According to the tests which Young made, the liquid turned out to be a high quality mineral oil subsequently rejected as not significant enough by the authorities within the chemical works.

Young's next move was to open a small refining works near Alfreton in Derbyshire where the oil had originally been found. However, the stream dried up, Nevertheless, having reasoned that this oil might be derived from coal, Young set to work to examine different types of coal in order to discover which should provide the greatest yield. It transpired that a sample, sent by an old acquaintance, Hugh Bartholomew, proved particularly high in oil when heated. It came from Bathgate.

This "parrot coal" was mined by Young from a coalfield belonging to Gillespie. This gentleman decided, since the coal was not being sold in the usual way, to demand from Young a larger share in the profits. Young refused. The law case which ensued was settled in August 1853 in his favour. He switched his attentions to shale, in the area of Bathgate: coal produces a greater yield of oil, but the supplies of shale were limitless.

The paraffin oil which he marketed for lamps gave Young his nickname. His patent expired in 1864 and other firms started to produce the oil, expanding Broxburn, Pumpherston, Mid Calder and West Calder and complete villages grew up around the new shale mines—Winchburgh, Niddrie, Seafield and Addiewell. Soon, however, imported American oil was cheaper than the home-grown product but by this time Young was manufacturing candles. Amongst other types of oil, petroleum jelly, wax for beekeepers and a special fluid for powering lighthouse lamps proved economical; paints, rubber goods and even mothballs were manufactured as by-products of shale oil.

At the beginning of the First World War the number of companies refining shale oil had been reduced from ninety to seven, and after the war they merged under the government-controlled Anglo-Persian Oil Company in the name of Scottish Oils Limited. The end of the shale industry came in 1962: it has been estimated that there is still 300,000,000 tons of shale to be mined.

James Young used to help David Livingstone financially with his missionary work in Africa and he also entertained the famous explorer, former student contemporary, at Limefield House. The miniature Victoria Falls and the sycamore tree which Livingstone constructed and planted are still to be seen in the grounds of the house. Paraffin Young's legacy lies under the ground.

LORD COCKBURN (1779–1854)

Henry Cockburn was born in Edinburgh, probably in the Parliament Close, and like Scott was educated at the High School and the University. At the latter, again like Scott, he studied law.

In 1806 he was appointed an advocate-deputy as a result of his Tory relatives' influence (the Tories were then in power), but Cockburn was a Whig of Whigs and when he showed this, he was dismissed.

In 1811 he married and settled at Bonaly in the Pentlands. He became one of Scotland's two leading advocates, and excelled as defence counsel in criminal cases (e.g. at the trial of Burke and Hare).

Cockburn was a reformer both of law and parliament, and anonymously produced many noteworthy pamphlets and articles. With the election of a Whig Government in 1830 he became Solicitor-General for Scotland and was chiefly responsible for drawing up the Scottish Reform Bill. In 1831 he was elected Lord Rector of Glasgow University and three years later he became, as Lord Cockburn, a judge of the court of session. By 1837 he was a lord of justiciary.

Two years before his death Cockburn brought out his "Life of Lord Jeffrey" (his fellow-student, fellow-advocate, fellow-judge and fellow-Whig, who died 1850). But the works he wrote which are still most read were to appear posthumously. The famous autobiography of his earlier life, "Memorials of His Time" came out in 1856, and records in a most lively, graphic and readable manner the outstanding characters and changes in society he had noticed before 1830. The "Journal . . . 1831–44" which was a sequel appeared in two volumes in 1874.

In the "Memorials" he recalls from his boyhood the ancient Edinburgh grande

dame, Lady Arniston:

"She was generally to be found in the same chair on the same spot; her thick black hair combed all tightly up into a cone on the top of her head; the remains of considerable beauty in her countenance; great and just pride in her son (Lord Melville); a good representative in her general air and bearing of what the noble English ladies must have been in their youth, who were queens in their family castles, and stood sieges in defence of them. Lady Arniston was in her son's house in George Square when it was attacked by the mob in 1793 or 1794, and though no windows could be smashed at that time by the populace without the inmates thinking of the bloody streets of Paris, she was perfectly firm, most contemptuous of the assailants, and with a heroic confidence in her son's doing his duty. She once wished us (schoolboys) to go somewhere for her on an evening; and on one of us objecting that if we did our lessons for next day could not be got ready —'Hoot man!' said she, 'What o' that? As they used to say in my day—it's only het hips and awa' again.' . . ."

It is interesting to compare this with Carlyle's description of Cockburn himself: "rustic Scotch sense, sincerity and humour, all of the practical Scotch type . . . small, solid and genuine . . . a bright, cheery voiced, hazel-eyed man; a Scotch dialect with plenty of good logic in it, and of practical sagacity; veracious, too. A gentleman, I should say, and perfectly in the Scotch type, perhaps the very last of that peculiar species."

Lord Cockburn: *Detail from a portrait in the Scottish National Portrait Gallery*

SIR WALTER SCOTT
(1771–1832)

Scott was a figure of world significance in the history of the novel, and is still hugely popular today.

Born in College Wynd, Edinburgh, the son of a Writer to the Signet, he was educated at the High School and University of his native city. In 1792 he was called to the Bar.

The young lawyer was a great reader and collector of ballads, and "The Minstrelsy of the Scottish Border" (published 1802–3 by James Ballantyne of Kelso) was his first important publication. At this time Walter Scott was sheriff-deputy of Selkirkshire.

Between 1805 and 1817 he brought out his verse romances, such as "The Lay of the Last Minstrel", "Marmion" and "The Lady of the Lake". But the meteoric rise of Lord Byron put Scott in the shade as a popular versifier.

In 1814 he published, anonymously, his first novel, "Waverley", which scored an astonishing success. The great series known as the Waverley Novels followed (also anonymously until 1827). These included "Guy Mannering", "The Antiquary", "Old Mortality", "Rob Roy", "The Heart of Midlothian" and "Redgauntlet".

James Ballantyne and his brother John had set up in Edinburgh as publishers, and Scott had become a partner. In 1811 Scott bought Abbotsford on the Tweed and built a large and expensive house there, which still exists today, largely as a Scott museum.

There he lived with his family and enjoyed playing the Border laird. But in 1826 James Ballantyne and Co. became involved in the bankruptcy of Constable and Co. and Scott nobly took upon him-

Sir Walter Scott: *Detail from a portrait in the Scottish National Portrait Gallery*

elf the task of paying off a debt of £114,000 with his own writing. This crushing burden certainly shortened his life.

Walter Scott read widely and had a phenomenal memory. A vast amount of learning is incorporated in his historical novels, which also contain much spectacular action, elaborate set-pieces and some memorable characters.

In 1820 Scott was created a baronet. Two years later came his hour of supreme glory as a public figure, when he stage-managed the visit of King George IV to Edinburgh. Today a statue of the King in George Street, and George IV Bridge remind us of that visit.

Walter Scott loved his native city passionately and knew it intimately. Here is the famous passage from Chapter VIII of "The Heart of Midlothian" where he recalls his favourite walk, high above Auld Reekie:

"If I were to choose a spot from which the rising or setting sun could be seen to the greatest possible advantage, it would be that wild path winding around the foot of the high belt of semi-circular rocks, called Salisbury Crags, and marking the verge of the steep descent which slopes down into the glen on the south-eastern side of the city of Edinburgh. The prospect, in its general outline, commands a close-built, high-piled city, stretching itself out beneath in a form, which, to a romantic imagination, may be supposed to represent that of a dragon; now, a noble arm of the sea, with its rocks, isles, distant shores, and boundary of mountains; and now, a fair and fertile champaign country, varied with hill, dale, and rock, and skirted by the picturesque ridge of the Pentland mountains. But as the path gently circles around the base of the cliffs, the prospect, composed as it is of these enchanting and sublime objects, changes at every step, and presents them blended with, or divided from, each other, in every possible variety which can gratify the eye and the imagination. When a piece of scenery so beautiful, yet so varied,—so exciting by its intricacy, and yet so sublime,—is lighted up by the tints of morning or of evening, and displays all that variety of shadowy depth, exchanged with partial brilliancy, which gives character even to the tamest of landscapes, the effect approaches near to enchantment."

SIR JAMES YOUNG SIMPSON (1811–1870)

Simpson hailed from Bathgate, where his father was the village baker. His brilliance revealed itself at the local school, and his father and six elder brothers united to finance his higher education at Edinburgh University. He began in the arts classes at 14, but from 1827 he studied medicine, graduating five years later.

James Simpson's outstanding ability continued to be recognized, and at 28 he was professor of midwifery at Edinburgh. Anxious to relieve his patients' sufferings, he was greatly interested to hear of the discovery of ether anaesthesia in the

Sir James Young Simpson:
Detail from a bust in the Scottish National Portrait Gallery

U.S.A. by W. T. G. Morton in 1846. As early as January 19th of the following year Simpson used it at a birth. He was the first to do so.

Simpson discovered, however, that ether was not the answer, and he experimented with other possibilities. Until now chloroform had been taken only internally, but on November 4th, 1847, in his house at 52 Queen Street, Edinburgh, Simpson and two other doctors inhaled chloroform as an experiment. Some time later their inert bodies were discovered on the floor. It worked!

Simpson publicly demonstrated the efficacy of chloroform as an anaesthetic a fortnight later. This, however, turned out to be the start of a lengthy and bitter battle. Many people, including ministers of religion, were passionately against this use of chloroform. It was felt that the avoidance or prevention of pain was somehow unnatural, harmful and against God's will.

Queen Victoria's views became known when she allowed chloroform to be employed to ease the birth of Prince Leopold in 1853. So deeply was she respected that this silenced all opposition.

The discovery of chloroform was far from being Simpson's only achievement. He practically founded gynaecology and made great advances in obstetrics. He was also an outstanding advocate of hospital reform. He won many honours, became a D.C.L. of Oxford in 1866 and in the same year was made a baronet.

Sir James died at his home in Queen Street, and is buried (by his family's wishes) in Warriston Cemetery, Edinburgh, and not in Westminster Abbey. The Maternity and Simpson Memorial Hospital in Edinburgh was erected with money contributed by a host of Simpson's friends.

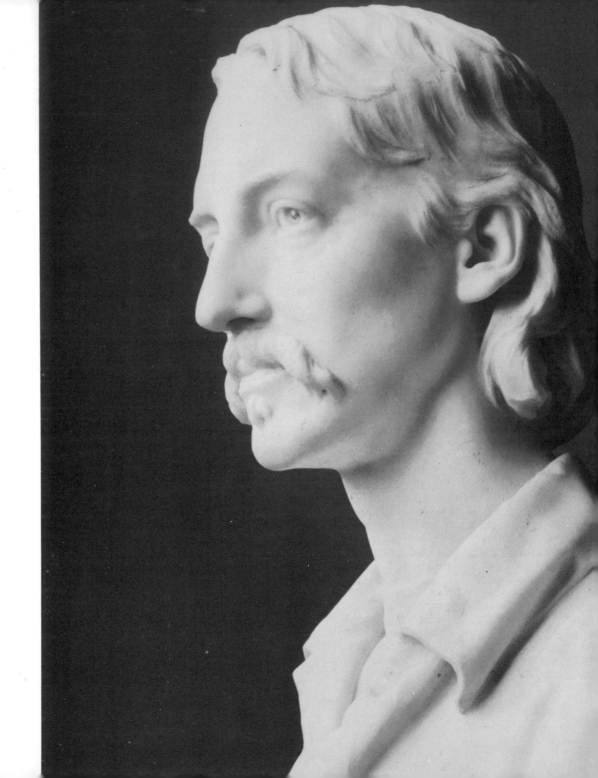

Robert Louis Stevenson:
Detail from a bust in the
Scottish National Portrait Gallery

ROBERT LOUIS STEVENSON (1850–1894)

Stevenson was born at 8 Howard Place, Edinburgh. He went to various schools (including Edinburgh Academy) but his health even then was frail, and he had little sustained schooling. And anyway he preferred to attend the school of life.

At Edinburgh University he studied (in his family's tradition) engineering, and then (like our other two authors) law, but he practised neither. As he always understood, his life was to be devoted to literature.

At first supported by his family, Stevenson launched himself on a literary career, reading a great deal and imitating the writers he admired. Then and later he travelled much for his health (he suffered most of his life from tuberculosis).

In 1880 Stevenson married the American divorcée Fanny Osborne, who became his devoted nurse and helpmate. On his father's death in 1887 he and his entire household left Scotland for good. After travels in the Pacific, Stevenson settled with them in Samoa, where he involved himself politically on behalf of the natives. He died there of a cerebral haemorrhage and is buried on Mount Vaea, near Vailima, his last residence.

Stevenson's most widely-read books include "An Inland Voyage" and "Travels with a Donkey" (travel); "Virginibus Puerisque" (essays); "Treasure Island", "Kidnapped", "The Master of Ballantrae", and "Catriona" (historical romance); "The Child's Garden of Verses" (childhood reminiscences); "Dr. Jekyll & Mr. Hyde" (horror); "The Ebb Tide" (one of his tales of the Pacific) and the uncompleted "Weir of Hermiston", a Scottish novel of dynamic power and profound insight.

"R.L.S." spent years perfecting his own taut and muscular style. Like everything else about his writing, it intimately reflects the man himself. He is one of the most personal of authors.

Whatever he wrote—novels, essays, short stories or verse—it is his attractive, lively, gallant and generous personality that shines through the result. To a million children, and to all the young in heart, Stevenson remains the "unseen playmate" of one of his own poems.

In this book it is appropriate to quote his vision of Lothian as seen from his beloved Pentlands. It comes near the end of "Edinburgh: Picturesque Notes".

"All around (Edinburgh), cultivated fields, and woods, and smoking villages, and white country roads, diversify the uneven surface of the land. Trains crawl slowly abroad upon the railway lines; little ships are tacking in the Forth; the shadow of a mountainous cloud, as large as a parish, travels before the wind; the wind itself ruffles the wood and standing corn, and sends pulses of varying colour across the landscape. So you sit, like Jupiter in Olympus, and look down from afar upon men's life. The city is as silent as a city of the dead: from all its humming thoroughfares, not a voice, not a footfall, reaches you upon the hill. The sea-surf, the cries of ploughmen, the streams and the mill-wheels, the birds and the wind, keep up an animated concert through the plain; from farm to farm, dogs and crowing cocks contend together in defiance; and yet from this Olympian station, except for the whispering rumour of a train, the world has fallen into a dead silence . . . but to the spiritual ear, the whole scene makes a music at once human and rural and discourses pleasant reflections on the destiny of man."

CHAPTER 4

AGRICULTURE

William Cobbett entered East Lothian on one of his Rural Rides in 1832, and he saw "such cornfields, such fields of turnips, such turnips in those fields, such stack-yards as never, surely, were before seen in any country upon earth." Cobbett was coming into the Lothians at the East end, at Cockburnspath; and even today the journey towards Edinburgh evokes feelings, if not as fulsome as Cobbett's, at least of admiration, of the farming potential. After the Union of Parliaments in 1707, some Scots lairds saw the developments in the South, the improvement of the land by draining, liming and the rotation of crops. The lairds and their tenant farmers were also able to read about "improvements" in farming journals, and some of them determined to imitate their southern brothers. The more northerly climate gave sufficient heat and light for the crops, but allowed fewer insects and diseases to develop. It would be pleasant to think too that the Scots of those days were enterprising and clever and hard-working enough to take advantage of their tutors' help and go ahead—but it might just be that having been used to a harder life, they continued their habits when the newer ways came along.

The great Revolution in farming during which so much drainage was done, brought all the most fertile lands in the Region into production by the mid 1800s. Before then it had only been possible to grow crops on sloping soil of lighter texture—now with a "rumbling stone" drain or a hollow 3″ pipe of clay, spaced usually at 6 yard intervals and $2\frac{1}{2}$ to $3\frac{1}{2}$ feet deep, dug into the ground wherever there was not a porous subsoil, the scene was set for the roots of crops to develop and to use the lime that sweetened the soil and the fertility provided by the animal and crop residues, as well as by the "artificial" fertilisers, just starting to come in. Of course the whole Regional area of today was not, nor is, suitable for the type of high farming that so impressed Cobbett. But the drains were a pre-requisite to it where it was and is practised, in nearly all locations. Though some of these drains are not now in prime condition, many still are—and those that have failed must be renewed if there is to be continuing success. Notice today for instance how few ditches there are here—for those early men knew that dry ditches silt up and need continuing care—so they built underground conduits of stone, often big enough for a man to crawl down; or later on put in big 6″ or larger pipes to take all drainage to running streams—thus ensuring as far as they could that short-term neglect would not in the far future endanger the success of their hard work. And it was hard work digging out the heavy clay subsoil to a depth of about 3 feet for mile after mile of drain-track!

In rough terms the Lothian Region is 56 miles long and averages about 13 miles wide; with a slight bulge to the North at North Berwick and one to the South in the Moorfoot hills below Edinburgh. Again to generalise, there is a strip of ground $6\frac{1}{2}$

A "Rumbling Stone" drain

miles wide on the North side for more or less the whole length of the Region that is pretty good from the farming point of view and comes into the classification of drained ground; while the parallel area of a further 6½ miles width to the South, plus the bulge into the Moorfoot hills, is really upland or hill ground. Of course one type merges into the next, but if we say that 0–500 feet is lowland, 500–1000 is upland and over 1000 feet is hill, we might, for most of this area, have a reasonable distinction, although the wetter conditions in the far West part of the Region bring the line down to a lower level. This land has a quite different agricultural value and suffers from the same disadvantages as the wider spaces of the North and West of Scotland. Of course most of the building going on in the area is on the lower ground, so there is a constant need to improve poorer ground if production is to be kept up—for instance in Midlothian alone 25 000 acres have been lost to Agriculture and Horticulture since 1918.

In the middle of the last century, the heyday of "improved" farming, all the agricultural land belonged to estates, most of which were managed with a strong feeling for the land, and for its possible returns. The estates were laid out into well-considered farms, which were let on long leases of up to 21 years. The advent of the turnip, clover and soon afterwards the general cultivation of potatoes, combined to provide the world-famous East Lothian six course rotation of yesteryear—and it was said that one farmer could even tell that a Golden Wedding date was inaccurately observed because he could remember that "that field in the front was barley that year". The rotation, (not as strictly observed in higher areas as in the most fertile parts) was Potatoes—Wheat—Turnips—Barley—One-year Ryegrass and

Potatoes

Turnips

Above: Wheat
Below: Barley

Clover ley—Oats and then dung on the ground for potatoes again. As a means of making full use of good land, labour and inputs with a minimum risk of disease, labour peaks, falling markets and with the concomitant cattle and sheep providing plenty of interest and scope for management, this way of farming could not then have been improved upon. On higher ground, where cropping was still suitable, i.e. broadly over 500 feet in drier parts or lower further west, Oats, Turnips, Oats, a three year or longer ley was practised. There were other variations as well; but the pattern was retained broadly until the forties, when the decline of the horse (partly through the incompatibility of higher wages and slow speeds, but also because of Grass Sickness, a mysterious disease that brought sudden death or lingering illness to horses) and the advent of such machines as combine harvesters, and specialised potato equipment meant that farmers had to consider specialisation in fewer lines of production; this co-incided with scientific advances that made it unnecessary to keep crops so far apart to combat disease and weeds, and the Government's contribution of Guaranteed prices took away, to a great extent, the old worries that high-cost arable farmers felt when most of their eggs were in vulnerable and few baskets. That the full-time labour force in Farming has gone down from 4600 to 2500 between 1962 and 1974 demonstrates too that, had the old methods continued, then there could not have been the completely justified rise in farm wages (relative to other workers) from around 30/- per week in 1930 to the levels of today, when for similar hours, better amenities and less laborious toil the pay is around £50 per week. The farm worker of yesteryear was a man with many hard-won skills at his command—a man who could

scarcely count the interest and perquisites of his job as adequate consolation for the privations and exacting nature of his duties; and while some of the ablest farmers did well in the trade, many for long periods after 1879 (when prairie grain and refrigerated meat imports started to flood into the country) also had a very thin time—and both suffered under the policies of importing bargain foods wherever in the world there was surplus— and only gained when War, or other disaster, led to shortages. With less workmen today and much machinery, the employee who can calculate and judge with commonsense and study the instructions book, is the man needed—not the proverbial "strong in the arm, weak in the head" type who admittedly had a place long ago! The skills do not need perhaps so much practice to achieve tolerable standards, but they demand judgment in exercising them that was not required before.

In the West of the Region the Rainfall

Turkeys at Fenton Barns

is around 50″—in the Eastern extremes it averages about 22″. But unlike South England the rates of evaporation are not so high—and if crops are sown well (and varieties with good root systems are chosen), then results are pretty predictable even if a dry season ensues. By this is meant that grain yields in East Lothian can be predicted for any well-run farm as say 12% up or down from normal for any but a freak year—and such years seldom come—in fact never have on the writer's farm: the 1976 drought had not nearly such a severe effect in East Scotland as further South, and although some farmers have irrigation equipment this is more to

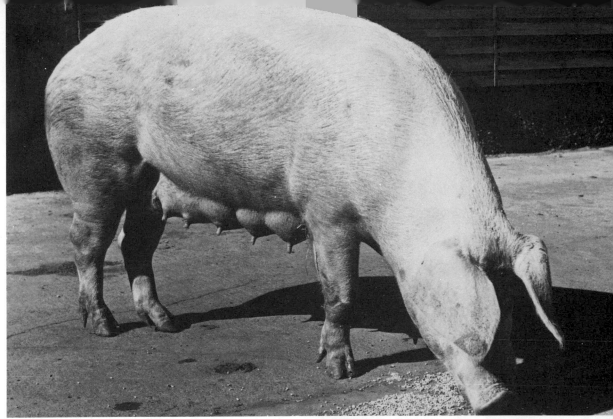

enable them to grow early potatoes even earlier and better or to keep cows on grass acreages that would otherwise be too low to guarantee success in usual operations.

Much of the ground in the Edinburgh area, where horticultural crops have long been grown, has a moisture retentive capacity, partly built up over the years from heavy dressings of dung from city sources, that means little need for extra water which would only make the soil colder.

The pattern of the farms in the arable areas within 6 or 7 miles of the Sea (with the exception of a small section in the far West where dairy farming still has a strong hold) is of 300 acres or so, mostly held as one unit only and more probably owner-occupied than now part of an Estate. The farmer probably has two men or three to help him—he perhaps grows about 170 acres of barley, 50 acres of wheat, 40 acres of potatoes and has 40 acres of leys with perhaps some turnips to fatten cattle on in the wintertime. He is likely to have no special output of pigs, poultry etc. since such production has now become very specialised—and is either carried out as separate departments on large farms or on farms devoted entirely to them. An example of this is to be found at Fenton Barns, near Drem, where turkeys are produced on a big scale under the banner of British United Turkeys, itself largely built on the initiative of the farmers there. Again, in pursuit of further challenges, a pig unit at Fenton to bring the progeny of 500 resident sows to maturity has been added to the complex, as has a large laying hen unit; which all proves that where more than the back of an envelope is needed for data to manage an enterprise, no one can say how anyone will fare till he starts—but when he does, if he has initiative, enough resources to get things rolling and the

Above left: Cabbages
Above: Brussels sprouts
Left: A field of leeks

Spraying a field of Strawberries

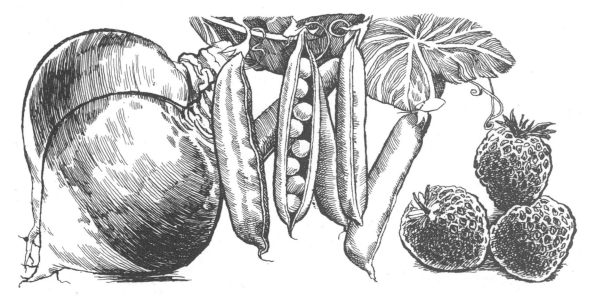

project appeals to him, then success is much more likely to breed success than bring too much difficulty on itself. Horticultural production, either for the fresh market or for processing is another possibility for an enterprising man whose farm lends itself to such things—in this case the farmer may not have cattle, since livestock can compete with greens for the attention that both may need; and, perhaps it is wistful to say so, but the manure coming from the cattle does not now have the aura that it once enjoyed as a sine-qua-non of market-growing. Along the East Lothian coastal fringe, hard white cabbages, now in much demand in the Spring for Coleslaw production as well as to eat in the ordinary way, have been found to survive the winter successfully, and since they must be well grown by November to be usable in April, this provides one possible crop for some favoured farmers. Others grow sprouts, leeks, turnips and swedes, carrots etc. for sale mainly in Glasgow and Edinburgh markets and they provide a high proportion of the produce there; peas and sprouts are also sent to the Elba Co-operative factory at Eyemouth from East Lothian. Soft fruit is mainly strawberries, produced around Haddington on smaller holdings there where the soil and conditions have proved good enough to keep some 200 acres in this rather exacting form of production. Barley crops are mainly grown with the hope of achieving a malting outlet at harvest—for a large market is on hand in the Edinburgh breweries' needs. Short strawed varieties with high yields, some predispositions to disease (this incurs expensive treatments, particularly for mildew) and a much better chance of not being beheaded by harvest-time gales, give current average yields varying up to 2 tons per acre. Wheat, grown in Scotland mainly near a potato crop or

Grazing

after a long ley, can better that yield, but not by much—and in fact the benefits of putting in wheat rather than barley are probably real, but much less than in South England where sun favours the wheat and even more dire diseases can detract from the barley. Wild oats have "got away" in a few places where runs of cereals have been prolonged—but the realisation of the menace has now come to all and only the most shortsighted or poorly pursed do not act to reduce by spray or pull.

While some irrigated early potatoes are grown round the coastline, to succeed the Ayrshire crop in the local markets, the main outlet is the Ware trade—i.e. the housewife is the customer. Dunbar area is particularly good for growing potatoes with a nice, red soil look; but since the advent of mechanical harvesters a few years ago, growers there have been at a disadvantage because they have had too much damage caused to the "more delicate than people think" skins of the spuds by rattling around with stones. The recent development of machines to riddle out the stones before planting and to put them all in lines between where the potatoes are grown so that they are not involved when the potatoes are lifted (except to provide a bit more stability for the wheels of the lifting machines) is a breakthrough that will have an effect here.

At all costs damage must be reduced to a minimum; and here the type of soil, the variety, the care taken in all operations are part of the process of getting as near to perfect as possible, allied to more and more complex machines with much of that complexity in softening the shakings and suffusing the scratches. Some potatoes are also grown for crisping (the Golden Wonder Company originated in Broxburn), although sugars can be higher in our cooler climate—however the latter conditions help to induce canners to take the higher moisture potatoes to factories further South for putting into tins.

The crops of the old rotation for selling straight off the farm were wheat, barley and potatoes—the oats, hay and turnips made up, with at times not inconsiderable quantities of cotton or linseed cake, rations mainly for fattening livestock: cattle and sheep, and the four or five pairs of horses that a 300 acre arable farm needed. Nowadays the oats are probably not grown at all, except up in the hills where lime status makes barley less likely to succeed. Barley unsuitable for malting can do more than oats for fattening an animal. The short term leys (for production, a one year Italian ryegrass can outyield anything else in terms of grass and make much better use of very expensive fertiliser) are used either for hay or silage,

Cattle housing

probably cut twice, then grazed thereafter, if fencing permits. Silage was much more easily mechanised than swedes in earlier years, but now the only difference is that swedes must still require the farmer to go into fields in winter. Otherwise feeders make up their own minds about how to organise the food, the bedding, the housing and the care of their cattle. Many cattle have been rehoused in new buildings as can be easily seen by passers-by. Other farmers have made clever adaptations to enable their old courts to be used in much more labour-saving ways—new building must emulate as far as possible the first class environmental conditions of the old (to use a "new" phrase), while reducing the work to a tenth of the old way! Cattle are now finished for the butcher much younger than in previous times—they have more muscle, which is more economical to produce, but which needs more high quality food to produce it—so the emphasis has to be on giving cattle the best, if the best results are to be obtained. Successful feeders take the job seriously and do not regard it as either a hobby or a chore.

Very few sheep are now fattened on low ground; but where the job persists, the animals still use their woolly coats to turn the elements—and are usually a lot happier than a passer-by would think in their sometimes muddy swede field, with about two minutes of gastronomic delight each day as they gobble up their half pound of corn for breakfast.

In at the farm will be a fairly sophisticated workshop, if the farmer is young, a grain store, a potato shed and other storage buildings, as well as a fork-lift truck, a front end loader and a series of tractors; there may well be two for each man regularly employed.

Such is progress—and no farmer can remain anything like self-sufficient today. The outlays go on, whatever we do, so we must have the income to put to them!

Dairying is conducted here and there on the lower ground, where either the idea to conduct it has entered the head of the participant, or where he has of choice decided to continue with it. The returns from a high output system have a certainty and are at a level that can make sense in economic terms, for today's dairyman regards his grass as a crop to be fertilised and managed and harvested (either by mouth or machine) and where better to do this than where other crops grow well?

But wherever it grows and whatever it is for, a grass sward must be made up of a maximum number of useful grasses and a minimum number of weeds (grass or otherwise).

There has been, as in other areas, a great swing in the Dairy world towards the British Friesian; for the production of calves as well as the realisation value at the end of a milking life are but two advantages—some may think otherwise, but the placid temperament and adaptability of the Friesian cow to her surroundings

Friesian Cows

mean that she is better suited to the modern methods of keeping cows in large loose-housed courts—and so, while there are enthusiasts who cannot be parted from their beloved true brown and whites, there are many who have changed over to the black and white; and particularly in the early stages when they have so many of their cows showing the blend of the two, they will have little to make them regret the change.

In the Southern part of the Region are Upland and true Hill farms. Upland farmers mainly breed cattle and sheep—some they fatten themselves, but mainly they confine their efforts to breeding, particularly with cattle. One reason is that the farmer on low ground who establishes a unit to do so can buy in stores to suit his purpose and achieve economies of scale, of uniformity and of location. The higher up farmer will have several lots of different sizes and they will be competing with their mamas for anything they get. Better probably to have more mamas (which the lowland man cannot do) and make a

An upland farm

cracking good job of their calves, so as to get them to the Sales with only six months to go before fat, so gaining a premium from feeders who only have one facility, either a summer or a winter operation. This is encouraged too by grants for breeding stock given now under EEC Regulations to less favoured areas, which are so helping to keep up production in the hillier areas—for this, in anyone's view, must be where the store stock should be bred. But experience has proved that,

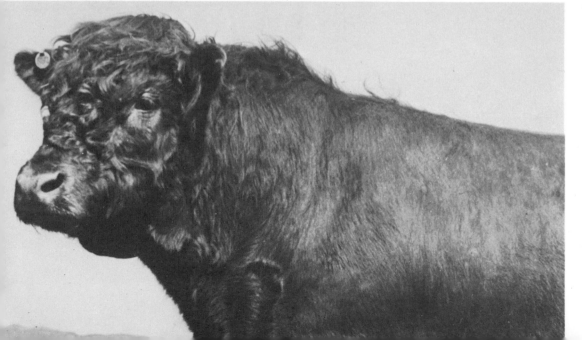

Above: the Highlander
Above left: the Blue-grey
Bottom left: the Luing

whatever the official bounty, it cannot pay to keep more cattle in the Hills than the farm is able to graze economically and provide the bulk winter-rations for. Cows are outwintered in sheltered areas of easily drained soil, or they are put inside from Christmas till April. Otherwise the ground suffers far more than the cows—always supposing the breed is right. The Galloway, the Highlander, the Luing, but mainly the

first, are the three breeds that are the foundation of most outwintered stocks of cows—Blue Greys (Cumberland White Shorthorn crossed with Galloway) as an outside breed or a Hereford cross (possibly with a Friesian) for inside are often used—then as a terminal sire for beef-calf production, the general choice is either a Charollais or an Aberdeen Angus—depending on whether one wants an extra £40 for the calf at a cost in food, calving problems and wear on the cow or an easier life with less return. The consensus is that no young man who is keen and active should neglect the former—but those who feel they deserve a respite need not be too much worse off at the end. Some with non-Hereford cows may prefer a White-faced bull—they too subscribe to the "lesser activity" section. Silage or hay must provide the bulk of the cows' winter rations and the calves get some creep feed to keep them on the move.

Above: Hereford cow and calves
Above right: Highland cow and calves
Right: the Charollais

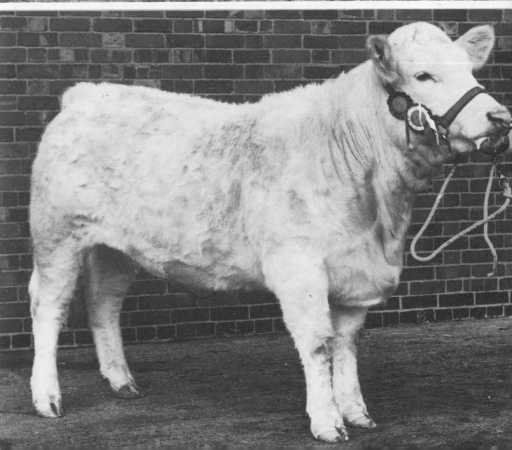

Blackface sheep

Top: Cheviots
Bottom: Greyface sheep

On the true Hill farms a few cows may be kept to scavenge around, but the main output is sheep and since in some cases the systems overlap, the sheep on hill and upland farms will be dealt with together. Most of the true hill flocks are Blackfaces, since most of the Hills are black (heather-covered) hills, as opposed to the green hills, more suitable for Cheviots. There these hardy sheep run and produce either pure-bred lambs or crosses by the Border Leicester—the wedders are fattened either on rape where they were bred or lower down—while a high proportion of the females either return to their native heaths to breed or, as crossed ewe hoggs, come down, often on to upland farms, to be mothers. One hill ewe per two acres is a reasonable stock rate. One hundred per cent lambing is what is wanted on higher hills where one single lamb successfully reared is better than a poor ewe and two poor progeny—while with half-breds (Border Leicester x Cheviot) or Grey Faces (Border Leicester x Blackface). a lamb and a half can be expected, or more. The economics of sheep were until recently poor—and in spite of greatly increased costs, the sale prices for lambs hardly rose at all for 20 years between 1950 and 1970. Recently with the opening of French markets and some scarcity because of the greater difficulty of getting New Zealand lamb into this country, there has been a great increase in the return from sheep and a much greater confidence about their future. As users of a minimum of expensive inputs and a maximum of home grown resources, their contribution to the profitability of a farm can be out of proportion to their gross return—and for this reason their production merits encouragement.

Trees for shelter

Forestry is not the subject of this chapter, but mention may be made of the value of trees for shelter. Trees do not grow quickly where the weather is often dry; and commercial forestry is not likely to be successful in the Region; but for amenity, shelter and to enhance the view (one cannot live off the view, but it is none the less an important aspect), trees are an indispensable part of the countryside. While hedgerow trees and some hedges have had to be pulled out in the interest of mechanised culture, our forebears have made such a good job of laying out the countryside that this particular kind of "despoliation" does not seem to have been as widespread or noticeable as in other parts of the country. But with our open cast coal mining, cement works, industrial sites, roads and houses etc., we are still losing a lot of ground; and it is necessary that no more than must be is taken away.

It is also important that those who are producing from the land do not have more restrictions put on their activities than is really necessary. The countryside has become what it is through the good efforts and foresight of our predecessors; the writer, a farmer, has had much help in his efforts to maintain the process, and puts in here a plea for a continuing official attitude of "if in doubt, allow".

How then does our Region compare today in its appearance and underlying quality of operations with the scene viewed by Cobbett nearly 150 years ago? Cobbett came when farming was in the midst of a period of prosperity—yet who could then feel secure with rinderpest or potato blight or even (if unlucky) eviction for little reason, ever a possibility?

Today farming here enjoys a stability and, for those established and competent, a security unknown then. But the intervening times have been hard indeed for farmers, workers, even for lairds. The coming of Science has made a huge difference to farming in all ways—it has brought the modern ways to farming and the work of the College of Agriculture has reduced the gap between the good and the bad farmer—for all now have access to all the knowledge and advice available. To that extent there is now less difference in methods and means; but farming being such a personally involved way of life there will always be the inspired practitioners, successors of Cockburn of Ormiston, Fletcher of Saltoun, the Sixth Earl of Haddington, Brown of Markle and many others who brought their methods towards the fruition that was so wonderful. No enterprise or area, no business or authority can ever with equanimity rest on its laurels—garlands go limp when their wearers do—but with a continuing Governmental policy of sometimes a nibble, but never a surfeit, of the carrot of good times, and no drastic changes in modern science (what would happen if food could be synthesised without roots and leaves and soil and toil?), surely our cornfields may continue to excite some favourable comment in the future, even if our stackyards, and our turnips, are by then a bit out of date.

Industrial Profile of the Lothian Region

WHERE THE PEOPLE ARE— Proportion of Regional Population	East Lothian	Mid Lothian	West Lothian	Edinburgh	
	10.4%	11%	15.8%	62.8%	
WHERE THE JOBS ARE— Proportion of Regional Workforce	7.5%	6.5%	14.2%	71.8%	
WHAT PEOPLE WORK AT— 1. Analysed by Region: Primary Industries	32.5%	34.5%	21.5%	11.5%	100%
Construction	8.5%	6.9%	16.5%	68.1%	100%
Manufacturing	7.3%	7.9%	28.4%	56.4%	100%
Service Industries	6.0%	4.1%	8.5%	81.4%	100%
2. Analysed by District: Primary Industries	17.6%	21.8%	6.2%	0.6%	
Construction	6.0%	8.5%	9.3%	7.6%	
Manufacturing	22.0%	27.9%	45.5%	17.8%	
Service Industries	51.4%	41.8%	39.0%	74.0%	
	100%	100%	100%	100%	
COMPOSITION OF WORK-FORCE IN THE DISTRICTS—Men —Women	63% 37%	65% 35%	66% 34%	55% 45%	
ABSOLUTE NUMBERS —People —Jobs	78,354 24,130	82,740 20,668	118,969 45,417	473,215 229,806	

CHAPTER 5

INDUSTRY IN LOTHIAN

The Imperial Dock, Leith

"Mercifully, Edinburgh has almost no manufactures; that is, tall brick chimneys, black smoke, or population precariously fed, pauperism, disease and crime, all in excess.

"Some strange efforts have occasionally been made to coax these things to us, but a thanks-deserving Providence has always been pleased to defeat them.

"For although manufactures be indispensable, they need not be everywhere. There should be Cities of Refuge."

Thus Lord Cockburn writing in 1849. Even now, nearly 130 years later, the eccentric comment of the author of the classic "Memorials of His Time" is quoted with a whiff of amused approval. Lord Cockburn s view has almost become part of the sub-culture and therefore it may be not too surprising to find that Lothian and industry are not exactly synonymous terms.

But whatever the facts may have been in Lord Cockburn s day—and even his admirers have admitted that he was occasionally partial to "striking adjectives and epithets"—Lothian is nowadays a substantial centre of modern industry.

And more than half of the people in Lothian who earn their living in industry are today employed in Lord Cockburn s "City of Refuge".

Lothian's industry used to be inelegantly, but accurately, described as banks, beer and books. The banks and the beer are still very important and so is the craft of the printer, even if publishing and papermaking are not nowadays what they used to be; but to those traditional activities has been added a whole range of modern skills, many involving high grade technology—electronics; heavy electrics; nucleonics; marine engineering; steel and non-ferrous founding; vehicle assembly; precision machining; food processing; textiles; the fabrication of metal and plastics; and—of course—manufacture of critical components for the North Sea: nodes and modules for production platforms, blow-out preventor stacks and, most recently, maintenance of well-head equipment.

That is a lengthy, but by no means complete, list. It illustrates the breadth of Lothian s industrial activity and the range of its skills. But it would be misleading to suggest that Lothian's potential for growth has been fully realised. A glance at the analysis of the employment structure indicates the resources of trainable labour. What is less easy to quantify is the ambience which Lothian provides for industrial development.

71

Two universities . . . the seat of Government in Scotland . . . a major sector of employment in professional and scientific services . . . a substantially higher proportion of the student age group receiving advanced education than the national average . . . and a physical environment which is endowed with most of the elements of grace. It is a formidable catalogue. To it the Region has added a major resource of land for industrial development. Throughout the Lothian Region there are 227 acres of fully serviced industrial sites and there are modern, single storey factories ready for immediate occupation. A further 1,250 acres are ready for future development in sites ranging from as big as 242 acres to as small as 2 acres.

This potential for development in Lothian—which so far provides 10,600 jobs on the Region's own industrial estates—is firmly founded on a com-

Above: Edinburgh Airport and (*left*) the interior

munications net-work which contains one of the key crossroads of modern Scotland —the junction at Newbridge, seven miles west of Edinburgh, giving access to the whole motorway net-work. No part of Britain is beyond overnight trucking distance.

The Regional airport at Turnhouse has recently been brought up to international standards and is capable of operating inter-continental flights. The seaport, at Leith on the Firth of Forth, can accomodate vessels up to 30,000 tons. There are, of course, main line rail links both north and south. How does all this work out in practice in stimulating high grade industrial development? There are many examples. Edinburgh Crystal is a traditional craft-based industry which developed its long established business with a bold move to a new greenfield site, involving a major investment in a new

Newbridge Interchange

factory, a new glass foundry and new plant and equipment. Microwave Electronic Systems Ltd., started in two condemned prefabs at a rent of £69 per year and now operates on an international scale from large, purpose built factories in two locations in Lothian. Nuclear Enterprises has built up a reputation in nucleonics and electronics which has attracted licensees for its designs and equipment from many countries, including the other side of the Iron Curtain. All of these are companies which started in Lothian, were nurtured by local enterprise and effort to the point where their reputations and their products are known, in their own fields, throughout the world. Perhaps it may be more significant to look in detail at a company which chose Lothian for a major development; at the reasons behind the choice; and at the progress the company has made.

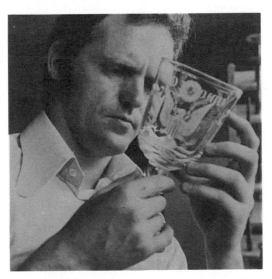

A craftsman examines a piece of Edinburgh Crystal

The Forth Road Bridge from the southern shore

73

Hewlett-Packard, the world wide electronics group, started in a garage in California in 1939 and now has a turnover of $1 billion. Hewlett-Packard's South Queensferry plant, which stands on a splendid area of rising ground looking across the Firth to the hills of Fife, is unique in the Hewlett-Packard organisation in that almost half of the electronic equipment which Hewlett-Packard produces at South Queensferry is designed and developed within the South Queensferry plant.

Left: Microwave and Electronic Systems factory
Below: Solid state Transmitter/Receivers for B.A. Trident automatic landing system

Testing a 140 MHz I. F. Microwave Link Analyzer

Hewlett-Packard Telephone Line Analyzer

Hewlett-Packard factory, South Queensferry

That is a remarkable tribute to the resource of high grade skills which Hewlett-Packard have been able to develop in Lothian and which they have not been able to achieve anywhere else in the world. The story was told in detail in the "Wall Street Journal" by the UK Managing Director, Mr. Dennis Taylor. It brings out so many features which make Lothian of interest for industrial development that it is worth examining in some detail.

Hewlett-Packard set up in Europe in 1959, with a UK operation in Bedford in 1961. The site was unsuitable for long term expansion and the company decided to look elsewhere. The basic requirements were a prime site capable of accommodating not only a facility which could eventually grow to 650,000 square feet, but would also permit the company to develop its own social and community philosophy; it needed an enthusiastic and trainable labour force; and it had to have first class communications for the despatch of parts and products as well as ease of access for the company's international clients.

The site also had to be within easy reach of universities to provide a source of graduate recruits and to permit university staff to be available on a consultancy basis.

Hewlett-Packard eventually chose its 33 acre site at South Queensferry. How did it work out? This is what the Managing Director wrote in the "Wall Street Journal."

"Local planning authorities gave every help in getting our project underway and the local banks were very helpful in providing the necessary finance. Industry already established in the area welcomed us and we operate in a very friendly and stimulating environment.

"Local labour was easily recruited and trained and we have continued to find an adequate supply of enthusiastic and diligent work people. Our labour turnover has been extremely low and we have a happy, contented and hard working group of people.

"Graduates have been recruited from the local universities and also from farther afield, since many enjoy working in the less crowded environment of Scotland. In addition to a source of local graduates we have further direct involvement with the universities. This takes the form of participation on advisory boards, providing specialist lecturers and working on specific research projects with members of university teams.

"Hewlett-Packard have been able to grow substantially over the past twelve years and our expansion has in every way met expectations."

That is a handsome tribute to a happy and successful development. What seems to emerge from it is that the physical advantages have to be right for a start, but qualities other than physical advantages are needed to attract modern technological industry. On the evidence of Hewlett-Packard's experience, Lothian seems to have the mixture about right. In the simplest terms it is a place in which industry finds it is a pleasure to live and to work.

In the remarkable variety of industry in Lothian, each district in the Region has its own distinct characteristics. Although Edinburgh still provides more than half of Lothian's jobs in the manufacturing industry, it has a large and very important component of service industry employment and one of the most significant sectors is banking, insurance, finance and business services. Edinburgh is widely known for its historical associations, but in strictly contemporary terms, Edinburgh is the financial power-house of the Scottish economy and is a centre of growing financial importance. Twenty per cent of the risk capital in the United Kingdom is managed from Edinburgh, which has the highest concentration of investment fund managers in the country outside London. Six of the nine mutual life insurance companies in Scotland have their headquarters in Edinburgh and some indication of the financial muscle which this represents is to be found in the total assets of the Scottish mutual life companies which now approach £3,000 million.

One of the best indices of the city's growing importance as an international financial centre is the remarkable increase in the number of foreign banks—mainly American—which have recently established operations in the city. Another is the growth of merchant banking, which has made available in Scotland the full range of corporate financial services that only a few years ago could not be obtained outside London.

Part of this development is no doubt

Canning plant, Scottish & Newcastle Ltd.
Opposite: Scottish & Newcastle Ltd., New Fountain Brewery, Fountainbridge, Edinburgh

due to North Sea oil but that has been only a make-weight reason for the foreign banks' decision to establish branches in the city. Fundamentally their assessment was that Edinburgh is a growth point of increasing financial importance in which they could not afford to be un-represented.

Brewing and printing have already been mentioned as major employers. Scottish and Newcastle Ltd. is one of the

Above: Cockenzie Power Station
on the Firth of Forth
Left: Cement works at Dunbar

Bilston Colliery near Edinburgh

big six breweries in the United Kingdom and the only one with its head office in Scotland. The company grew from the brewery established by William Younger in 1749, first at Leith and later in the vicinity of the Palace of Holyrood House. Now, in its huge new plant at Fountainbridge, Scottish and Newcastle have one of the largest and most fully automated brewing complexes in the world.

To the east of Edinburgh are the fertile agricultural lands of East Lothian. Although this is a predominantly rural area with splendid recreational facilities, it has its share of enterprising and highly successful industries. These include the volume production of small electric motors; high grade precision engineering; and the assembly of colour television sets. East Lothian has established a reputation as the place for thrusting local enterprise.

South of Edinburgh, Midlothian— which has a high proportion (20%) of its workforce employed in coal mining—has one of the most successful industrial development records in Scotland. Its manufacturing industries range through most of the standard industrial classifications and it has a labour force which has proved to be both diligent and trainable.

West Lothian has outstanding communications advantages. It is as easy to go west as east and with the whole motorway network at its door, there is no area of Britain to which there is not direct access. West Lothian has a very high proportion (46%) employed in manufacturing industries. It provides at Bathgate a location for British Leyland's truck and tractor plant employing 5,500 people.

British Leyland Truck & Tractor plant, Bathgate

In the new town of Livingston, in West Lothian District, the Region has a focus for major development. The town is already the second largest centre of population in the Lothian Region (24,000 people and growing at a rate of some 3,000 per year). The new town has been successful in attracting a wide range of industries, providing some 5,400 jobs in various manufacturing operations.

It will be obvious from all this that Lothian is a region of thriving industrial activity with great potential for further high grade development.

It will be obvious too that even if Lord Cockburn was right in his day, his views have been an unconscionable time a-dying.

Top left: Livingston Centre Shopping Centre
Bottom left: The Livingston Motec (Multi-occupational training and education centre)
Above: The Livingston Motec residential complex
Opposite: Livingston New Town

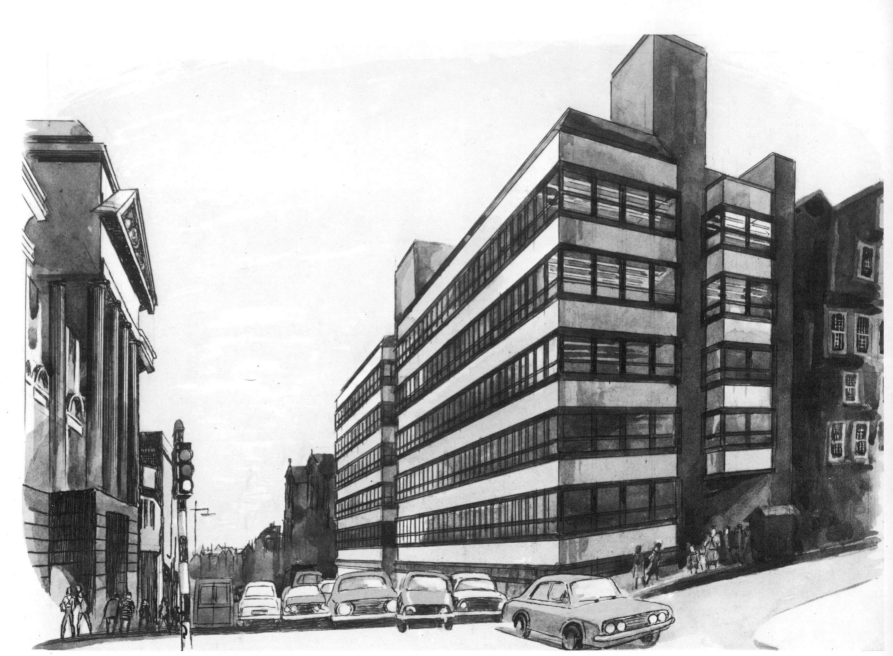

The Lothian Regional Headquarters, George IV Bridge

CHAPTER 6

GOVERNMENT AND THE COMMUNITY

Lothian Region with a population of 754,000 is the second largest of Scotland's new regional local government authorities.

The Local Government (Scotland) Act, 1973, replaced town, district and county councils with nine Regional Councils and 53 District Councils within the Regions. Lothian has four District Councils; Edinburgh, West Lothian, Midlothian and East Lothian, following generally the boundaries of the old city and county authorities.

The Regional Council with a budget in excess of £200 million has the major responsibilities—providing education, social work services, highways, drainage, police, fire fighting services, and water, for instance.

The major roles of the District Councils are the provision of housing and cleansing . . . but there are several responsibilities that are contiguous with those of the Regions, such as planning and recreation and leisure. The Regional Council pro-vides a strategic plan and the District Councils provide a detailed planning service within the regional strategy. The division of recreation services is not so clearly defined, but generally the Regional Council is involved with stimulation of the arts, development of countryside pursuits, sport and tourism; the District Councils manage sports grounds, swimming pools, parks, etc.

The Regional Council is served by one councillor elected from each of 49 divisions and the District Councils by two or more members from each of the divisions. Thirty-two Regional councillors are from Edinburgh, reflecting its importance in terms of population.

Elections to the Regional Council were held in 1974 and elections will therafter be held four-yearly. (Elections to the District Council were also held in 1974 and again in 1977; they will be repeated in 1980 and at four yearly intervals after that.)

The Leader of the Regional Council is known as the Convener and he is nominated by the elected members.

District Councils were allowed to continue the title of Provost, and the cities the title of Lord Provost, who is also Lord Lieutenant, the Queen's official representative.

Lothian Regional Council has some 36,000 employees, including teachers, police and firemen, and they function as a cohesive, corporate unit through the leadership of the Chief Executive.

Each Department has its own Director and the Directors sit as a Management Team to effect co-ordination and control of the Council's services. The Chief Executive is leader of the Team, and he is especially advised by an inner court of the Directors of Finance, Administration and Policy Planning, known as the Executive Office.

Their task is to apply resources to maximum effect to meet the political will of the elected Council.

District councils have similar management structures.

Education

Reorganisation also allowed for the setting up of Community Councils and School Councils to overcome problems of remoteness from the new bodies, and these have been established in Lothian. The Community Councils rely on the Regional and District Councils for funds and their purpose is to identify local issues. Schools councils in Lothian are being given an increasing role, including a voice in the selection of school senior staffs.

Local Government is big business, and the Education Department of Lothian Regional Council is alone a major industry. It has a revenue budget of more than £100 million and employs 19,000 people, 7,500 of them teachers. They run 45 secondary schools, 238 primary schools, 28 special schools for the handicapped, and a growing number of nursery schools . . . to accommodate 140,000 children.

Secondary school rolls number from 700 pupils up to 2,000 (Portobello High).

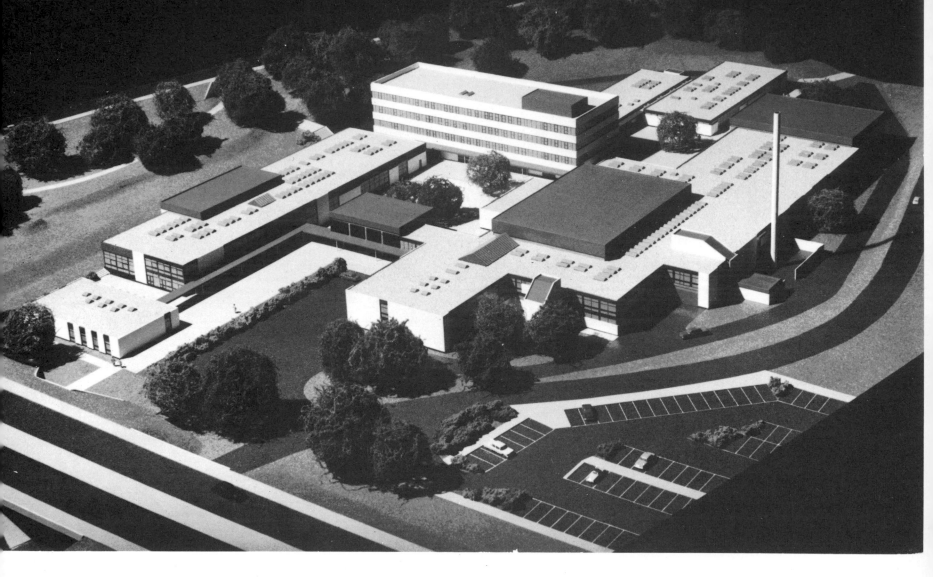

Model of Wester Hailes School,
Pool and Community Complex

An exciting new concept of the '70s is the School and Community Complex, and Lothian Region has the first at Wester Hailes, a new local authority housing development planned to have 5,000 houses. The £5 million complex includes a swimming pool, a community hall, library and study resource area, a lounge complete with a drinks licence and other community areas designed to serve 1,500 pupils and the local community. There are keep-fit and home economics classes for mothers, a creche, lunch club for the elderly, and practical activities for men on shift work. Evening activities are expected to develop to keep the complex as busy as during normal school hours.

A similar complex is being provided at Livingston new town, to serve the Deans community.

The Regional Council also has six colleges of Further Education; Napier, Telford and Stevenson in Edinburgh, the West Lothian College at Bathgate, Esk Valley College near to Dalkeith and the Oatridge Agricultural College. Napier makes provision for advanced level and degree courses (H.N.D. and C.N.A.A.) and Telford, Stevenson, Esk Valley and West Lothian provide craft and secretarial courses and the like, also making S.C.E. provision for people who have left school and wish to upgrade their basic school qualifications.

The Region also has two Universities, Edinburgh and Heriot Watt.

There are 27 private schools in the Region offering a full range of educational provision.

Social Work

Social Work, commanding an expenditure of some £25 million and employing 6,700 people, (2,600 of them full time), is perhaps the most complex of the Regional Council departments, providing a tailored service of social welfare advice, assistance, financial support, domiciliary care, day care, residential care and preventive work.

Merchiston Castle, Napier College, Edinburgh

The department aims to assist families to prevent break-ups, but also provides appropriate substitute care particularly of children. Assistance includes marriage guidance, advice on housing, money, drink problems, day care for children, support for playgroups, childminders and their registration, holidays for children, home helps and family aides and supervision of children in trouble, often referred by a Children's Hearing. It runs children's homes, recruits and supports foster parents and acts as an adoption agency.

Social Workers supply a hospital service, they can arrange for homes to be adapted for the handicapped and the department runs work training centres, workshops for the handicapped, clubs and day centres and employs occupational therapists.

It is an aim to keep the aged as independent as possible and social workers assist with arrangements for lunch clubs, day centres, meals on wheels, home helps, neighbourhood aides and wardens in sheltered housing schemes, but residential homes are run to provide full-time care where there is no alternative.

One social work team operates within Saughton prison. The department runs a hostel for recovering alcoholics.

Water

Lothian Region has a daily water consumption of 57 million gallons, equal to 75.5 gallons (343 litres) for every person. About a third of this goes to industry.

The water comes from 22 impounding reservoirs, 19 stream intakes and more than 260 springs, and it is augmented by nine million gallons a day from Loch Lomond that are piped across Scotland.

Responsibility for quality and distribution rests with the Water Supply Services Department of the Regional Council based mainly at Fairmilehead, Edinburgh, which employs more than 450 people.

Demand for water continues to grow and the council has embarked on a £30 million scheme to dam the Megget Valley in the Borders Region. The scheme will develop in two phases each providing an additional $22\frac{1}{2}$ million gallons of water a day and will satisfy anticipated demand well into the next century.

Sketch of the Megget Valley Dam

Transport

The Regional Council's Department of Public Transport operates a fleet of some 600 buses within the City of Edinburgh, and also maintains a fleet of about 1,000 miscellaneous vehicles owned by the Council. The buses are radio-linked to assist efficiency.

Drainage

Lothian Regional Council owns its own ship—MV *Gardyloo*, aptly named and most visible evidence of the operation since the beginning of 1978 of a new £35 million sewage scheme to serve more than two thirds of the city of Edinburgh. City sewage, discharged to the river for centuries, is now collected at Leith, separated at a rate in excess of 55 million gallons a day and its solids taken by ship to be dumped well out in the North Sea. Sewage is managed by the Department of Drainage which also maintains a watch on rivers and other watercourses to prevent flooding and is responsible for the inspection of coast protection works and dealing with oil pollution on beaches.

Planning

Strategic planning is a major Regional function and the Department of Physical Planning is responsible for the production of a framework of proposals for land-use—the development and improvement of the environment—and for the management of traffic. A first structure plan concentrates on the pattern of settlement, location of industry and employment, on mobility of the population and transport and on use of the countryside. The department co-ordinates Regional and District planning on matters of strategic development control and implementation.

Public transport in Edinburgh

Recreation

The Department of Recreation and Leisure is responsible for strategic initiatives to assist public and commercial operators plan for the future in terms of the countryside, art, tourism and provision for sports and physical recreation. It promotes Lothian throughout the UK and abroad as a major tourist destination.

The department manages two important regional facilities in the Pentland Hills: Hillend Ski Centre that attracts more than 100,000 skiers annually, and the Pentland Hills Country Parks.

It also advises the Council on the distribution of scholarships and grants to support individual talent in art and sports, and regional cultural bodies such as the Royal Lyceum Company.

Top left: Hillend Ski Centre
Centre: Summer in the Pentlands
Bottom: Winter in the Pentland Hills Country Parks

Consumer Protection Officers monitor trading standards and see their role as a referee enforcing rules to ensure that a correct balance of power is maintained between parties in trading transactions. They operate the traditional weights and measures service, control of food standards and safety standards for poisons and volatile substances, but a growing service is that of Consumer Advice. The department has a Consumer Advice Centre in Frederick Street, Edinburgh, giving free pre-shopping and complaints advice.

There is also a mobile Consumer Advice caravan that tours main shopping centres in towns and villages throughout the Region.

The remaining Service departments of the Regional Council are concerned with Property Assessment and Electoral Registration and with the Children's Panel. The operation of Children's Hearings, that took over the work of the old style juvenile courts, is a Regional function and is headed by the Reporter. Children alleged to have committed offences and those in need of protection are referred to the Reporter who will arrange for a Hearing by three members of the Panel. There is a close liaison with the departments of Education and Social Work.

Other departments of the Regional Council supply Central Support Services, such as Administration, Architectural services, Personnel, Finance, and also involve specialists such as the Estates Surveyor, the Public Analyst, Medical Assessor, Industrial Development Officer and Public Relations Officer.

A central service new with the reorganised system of local government is Policy Planning, whose Director is a member of the Executive Office. This service co-ordinates the forward thinking of all departments on all aspects of council work and advises on priorities.

The Director of Policy Planning also controls an Industrial Development Department, whose task is to establish and manage industrial estates and actively to promote the advantages of the Region for the development of industry, particularly manufacturing industry.

Joint Boards

The two emergency services—the Police and the Fire Brigade—function jointly for Lothian and for the Borders Region and their policy-making bodies are joint Boards of Management of which Councillors from each authority are members.

Headquarters for both services are in Edinburgh where the Chief Constable and the Firemaster exercise operational control.

A Joint Board also manages the Forth Road Bridge, this time of members of the Regional Councils of Lothian and of Fife.

Over page:
Dugald Stewart's Monument, Calton Hill, Edinburgh

CHAPTER 7

LOTHIAN AT PLAY

Lothian is industrial, agricultural and urban, and displays, at every turn, evidence of her past. Traprain Law was first examined methodically by Sir James Young Simpson. However, the discoverer of the anaesthetic properties of chloroform was not searching for Saxon loot, but for the grave of King Loth. Legend has it that Loth was slain by a shepherd who was in love with the King's daughter, Thenog. The result of this love between shepherd and princess was the child Kentigern, later Saint Mungo.

But the Kingdom of Loth is also a playground. For both visitor and native there is much to be enjoyed. The combination of the past and of the natural properties of the countryside have been welded together by human agency—in the form of private and public bodies—to form a whole to be enjoyed by everyone.

The countryside is rich and changing, offering pastoral and sportive delights. Many of the towns are charming. Edinburgh flavours the region with a massive dose of civilization; and the sea, which borders the whole northern length of Lothian, adds yet another characteristic to the region.

Winter, Gladhouse, 1962 *by Sir W. G. Gillies. R.S.A.*

The Pentlands, so beloved by Henry Cockburn, and his especial playground, are the most interesting hills in Lothian. They begin in the west and stretch for 12 miles eastward into Edinburgh itself. At Habbies Howe, on the south-eastern side, Cockburn conducted his annual breakfasts. It is also a spot associated with Allan Ramsay's "The Gentle Shepherd". Traditionally one of the barriers between North and South, the Pentlands, with their little river valleys cutting through them, hide the city beyond.

EDINBURGH AND LOTHIAN:

THE ARTS

The idea of "city-twins"—the establishment of friendship links between European communities of similar size and interest—may be a relatively new one, a post-war invention. Edinburgh claims kinship in this way with Munich and with Nice. But the concept of international parallel is much more ancient and in the last decade of the 18th century Edinburgh citizens in general and writers in particular proudly called their town "the Athens of the North". What was asserted was a claim no less than that Edinburgh provided leadership in taste, in artistic patronage and in intellectual advancement for Britain certainly, for northern Europe possibly.

In many ways Scotland's capital city still provides this leadership—in the arts with the continuing and highly reputed International Festival and with the presence of the great national collections, and in teaching and research with the growth of its University to a larger scale of operation than any other non-collegiate university in Britain.

No-one however can enjoy exposure to the stimulation of Edinburgh's cultural or intellectual life without realising how deeply rooted it is in the past, and in

Claudio Abbado conducting the London Symphony Orchestra at the Usher Hall during the 1977 Edinburgh Festival

particular in that 18th century past when the Scottish Enlightenment became one of the great influences in west European civilisation. To account for this is to bring into perspective the wealthy, agricultural lands of Lothian—the background against which fortunes could be formed, influence built and patronage exerted. Even in the 18th century proximity to Edinburgh and regular contact with the seats of law and political power were the essential ingredients of success for the

land-owning or professional classes. Nothing helped more than to have an estate large or small, handily placed for Edinburgh or at the very least a house in the Canongate or later in St. Andrews Square. Nothing was more likely than that this society of ambitious, open-minded, intellectually active and moneyed men should develop a cultural awareness and practice that spearheaded Edinburgh into a situation of artistic leadership. With funds from farms or coalpits or city banking,

Derek Jacobi in the Prospect Theatre's *Hamlet*, Edinburgh Festival 1977

hese lively generations travelled Europe —the Clerks came to Vienna, the Hopes o Naples and to Rome; they bought their Poussins and their Claudes, listened to the Bachs and to Corelli, and saw at first hand he Palladian villas of Vicenza. Taste, polished on the whetstone of the Grand Tour, was a matter of their everyday life and indeed a qualification essential to their advancement in political or managerial office.

The most obvious result of this aristo-cratic patronage in 18th century Lothian is of course the heritage of architecture. A century that was to start with William Bruce's classical Hopetoun and end with James Playfair's gothic Melville produced in Lothian more elegant great houses than any other period and more in Lothian than in most other areas of Scotland. After Bruce, Willam Adam's Arniston or Drum or John Baxter's Penicuik developed the Italian villa idea and Adam's colossal extension to Hopetoun House established a marriage between late baroque and the Palladian. Robert Adam produced New-liston and Archerfield, Seton and Oxen-foord but his finest work is in Edinburgh itself—at Charlotte Square, Register House and Old College. No-one indeed can adventure far into New Town Edin-burgh, from George Street—say—to the north, without being aware of the all-pervading influence of Adam—restraint, classical proportion, good composition.

The late Sir William Gillies R.S.A. in his studio, Edinburgh College of Art

In the 19th century the city gained embellishment from hands marginally less honoured than the Adams—W. H. Playfair ranging from the neo-classical at Surgeons' Hall to the Jacobean at Donaldson's Hospital, or William Burn or Archibald Elliot indulging in two neogothic churches at St. Paul's, York Place, and St. John's, West End. And later, if Edinburgh could not pioneer the modern movement with anyone like Glasgow's C. R. MacIntosh, at least it produced the staider attributes of Rowland Anderson. That the quality of architectural awareness is still much to the fore is shown not only by local government sponsorship—in the New Town—of the largest urban conservation area in any British city, but also by the regular and vitriolic debates over the future of the city's major gap sites or buildings erected to fill them. The Architectural Room in the annual Royal Scottish Academy Exhibition attests too the vigour of the ongoing practice.

The Royal Scottish Academy (itself a Playfair building) is one of the major centres of the Region's cultural life. Various societies and associations of artists regularly exhibit upon its walls and during the International Festival it accommodates special exhibitions of cardinal significance. When in April each year the Academy's own exhibition opens it seems like the symbol of a vanishing winter, the start of a new season of excitement, and Edinburgh turns out to see new work by familiar and unfamiliar hands. Patronage of painting through the Academy or through the various private galleries of the city has always been, and still continues, strong, and here again derives without any doubt from the inheritance of the past.

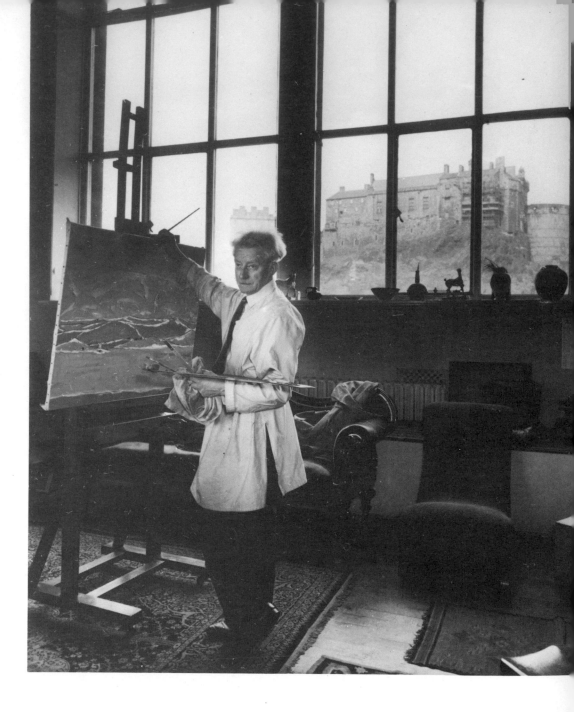

From the 17th century onwards, Edinburgh has been a centre for contemporary painting. Here a Lord Haddington would sit for Allan Ramsay, or a Lord Rosebery for Henry Raeburn. Here were to be seen —and bought—the works of David Roberts or Horatio MacCulloch, both living at Stockbridge, or—from his Lothian residence—the impressionist paintings of William MacTaggart. Today's Academy walls show the work of names no less famous but equally the product of the Edinburgh or Lothian environment— the landscapes of the late Sir William Gillies, living and working at little Temple village, or the canvases of Philipson or Houston, more Edinburgh centred. The Royal Scottish Academy and the Edinburgh College of Art together are two legs of a very healthy and active artistic body.

Left: Still Life (*top*) and Still Life, Yellow Table *by Sir William Gillies R.S.A.*

95

WORK BY
CONTEMPORARY ARTISTS
IN THE LOTHIAN REGION

Runswick Bay *by Elizabeth Blackadder*

Stone the Crows *by Sir Robin Philipson R.S.A.*

Short Cut *by Robert Callander*

Above: Park *by Anthea Lewis*
Below: Greens/Leaves *by John Mooney*

Above: Philipston Landscape *lithograph by Roy Wood*
Below: The New Member *by David Evans*

The Shining Calm of the Sea *pencil by Elizabeth Ogilvie*

Of course not all the great private collections of 18th century patrons remained in their private hands. At Hopetoun and other great houses that occasionally open their doors to the public one can find the typical collections of pictures, furniture and *objets d'art* of the enlightened aristocratic family. But many of these earlier treasuries were dispersed and it was this very dispersal that eventually provided the reservoir from which our great national collections came to be formed. In the National Galleries of Scotland, the Royal Scottish Museum and the National Museum of Antiquities Edinburgh possesses a wealth of painting, applied art and historic craftsmanship that cannot be rivalled by any other city of its size in Britain and by few others in Europe. The National Gallery is—by comparison with European galleries —small, but its rooms accommodate and display masterpieces of world importance —Vermeer, Velasquez, Van der Goes, Rembrandt and Poussin—presented in an area that produces neither fatigue nor aesthetic indigestion. It would be tedious to narrate here all the categories of craftsmanship contained within the Royal Scottish and National Museums: let it suffice to illustrate the theme of an inherited tradition by mentioning simply the elegance of 18th century Edinburgh silver that these museums house or of Edinburgh-Georgian furniture by makers such as Trotter. Today contemporary silverwork, glass-engraving, woodwork and textiles find a show-place, and indeed selling point, in the Scottish Craft Centre in the Canongate.

If the opening of the annual Academy marks the incipience of summer, the coming of autumn has its compensations with the regular series of wintertime

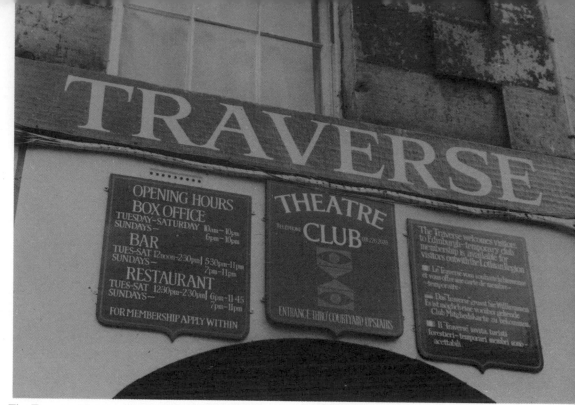

The Traverse Theatre, Grassmarket, Edinburgh

concerts provided by the Scottish National Orchestra, the Scottish Chamber Orchestra and the Scottish Baroque Ensemble together with other distinguished groups. The Usher Hall and the Freemasons Hall have since the opening of the century provided the main centres for musical enjoyment but a more adventurous spirit rules today. More intimate—may one say it, more attractive—environments for listening have been invoked. The Signet Library, a jewel of early 19th century decorative taste, occasionally accommodates recitals, the Scottish Baroque Ensemble regularly plays at Hopetoun and in the salons of other Lothian houses, and a new custom-altered concert hall is to appear in a former church.

But among the most delightful of settings is St. Cecilia's Hall, a classic oval taking about 200 of an audience to hear recitals in a building that links immediately—and yet again—with 18th century society. To read the nominal-roll of the mid-century "Edinburgh Musical Society" is to recite the names of half the land-owning or professional families of Georgian Lothian—the Clerks, the Dalrymples, the Hays and the Hopes— and they appear not only as patrons but also—occasionally—as composers. It is no small credit than in today's music shops you can buy on L.P. disc the compositions of Sir John Clerk of Penicuik, of David Foulis of Colinton and of the principal patron of the Society, the

Grassmarket: the old White Hart Inn, patronized by Burns and Wordsworth

A window was cut in the Flodden Wall at the top of the Vennel Steps in 1876

musical Earl of Kellie. And to St. Cecilia's Hall, where Edinburgh comes today, Edinburgh came then to hear Corelli or Tenducci, the Menuhin or Fischer-Dieskau in reputation of the time. Finally, to invoke the name of Menuhin is to remind ourselves of his intimate connection with "young music" at Haddington and to underline through this the flourishing entrepreneurship in the arts that exists there under the banner of "The Lamp of Lothian".

The theatre, one might well say, has often been a problem in Edinburgh. In the early 18th century attempts to set up a regular theatre in the town were strenuously opposed by the Kirk, and later in the 18th century performances could be upset by rioting servants or by Jacobite supporters. In the 19th century the Theatre Royal flourished for a time under Henry Siddons and later still its successor,

now in turn gone, was joined by the King's Theatre and by the Lyceum. Cultural hackles still regularly rise over the controversies surrounding the future of these playhouses—the height of contention centering upon the inadequacy of physical provision for Festival productions in a Festival City. Despite this, wonders are achieved; *Cosi* is no problem but to get a *Meistersinger* onto the King's stage is a major logistical triumph. At Festival time the apron-stage of the Assembly Hall has seen some high successes, not least that mainstay of former Festivals—the *Satire of the Thrie Estatis* by Sir David Lindsay.

There is an annual wonderment too at the ingenuity with which scores of visiting drama companies, enrolled under "the Fringe", adapt halls and compress productions into the most unlikely of physical situations. The Traverse Theatre, growing up in the Lawnmarket and settling into the

Grassmarket, pioneered a return to the ancient tradition by taking the theatre back up the close-mouth—where in Edinburgh it all started—and has provided Edinburgh ever since with some very untraditional entertainment.

On the Calton Hill stands Playfair's group of neo-classical buildings—an uncompleted Parthenon, a Lysicrates monument, a Temple of the Winds. In part they symbolise "the Modern Athens" and in part they commemorate great names associated with the 18th century awakening—Professor John Playfair, Professor Dugald Stewart—while David Hume is remembered in a Robert Adam mausoleum below. Adam too designed the Old College buildings to provide Enlightenment Edinburgh with a worthy "new University". And it is in the Old Senate Hall of this University that six masterpieces by Sir Henry Raeburn now hang. All this is simply to underline the intimate and important cultural association that exists between "the Toun" and "the Tounis College". No account of the arts in Edinburgh and Lothian could be complete without reference to the literary figures whom this interrelationship helped to produce.

Lothian indeed has provided the backdrop for so much literary inspiration. William Drummond, going back a century before the 18th, court poet to King James VI, lived precariously above the Esk at Hawthornden near Roslin; Allan Ramsay set his pastoral poem, *The Gentle Shepherd*, among the farms of Carlops; and Scott, spreading his life between Castle Street, a cottage at Lasswade and Abbotsford, invoked Edinburgh and Lothian most notably in *Heart of Midlothian* and in *The Bride of Lammermoor*. Poets Burns and Fergusson and novelist Susan Ferrier were more inspired by Edinburgh town-life, but R. L. Stevenson happily drew inspiration from Colinton Manse and Swanston Cottage. All these literary associations are well documented in the City's specialist museum at Lady Stair's House.

Inevitably such literary awareness produced periodicals of character and note. *The Edinburgh Review, Blackwood's* and *Chambers* all started in 19th century Edinburgh as avenues of criticism that brought together "the toun" (like Francis Jeffrey, advocate, judge and editor) and "the college" (like Professor John Wilson, *alias* Christopher North). Today the literary journal continues with spasmodic success, and today too Edinburgh and Lothian continue to give inspiration to poets and writers like Robert Garioch and David Daiches, to name but two.

Edinburgh people need make no excuses in claiming for their city and its region the cultural hegemony of Scotland. It is a fact incapable of separation either from the historical inheritance that produced it or from the promise and responsibility implicit in it for the years ahead.

SPORT AND PHYSICAL RECREATION

Lothian has excellent facilities for sport. With some 50 golf courses in the Region, wherever you live cannot be far from the carefully tended greens and rolling fairways. Golf has been played in Edinburgh since the 15th century. In order to play on a private course a recommendation from a member is generally required, but on the many municipal courses first class golf can be enjoyed at little cost.

The Regional Council is supporting an Old-fashioned Golf Project at Bruntsfield Links.

For fishermen Scotland has traditionally been an area of great importance and Lothian is no exception. Of particular interest is the problem of industrial pollution in the rivers and towns and with salmon living in the upper reaches of the River Almond it can only be hoped that similar activity will soon be seen in the Esk. The brown trout is native to Lothian and can be caught in the Dean Village. There can surely be few places in the world where fish can be caught in such pleasant surroundings so near to the centre of a city of such size. The opportunities for coarse fishing should not be

Above: Muirfield Golf Course, Gullane. *Below:* The Water of Leith

overlooked. Frequently permits are free and in principle there is no close season. Although coarse fishing does not enjoy the same respect and mystique as game fishing there is little doubt that there is tremendous potential for this sport.

In 1965 through the foresight and financial support of the late Mr. Boyd Anderson and the then Edinburgh Corporation, the largest artificial ski slope in Europe was created at Hillend in the Pentland Hills. (This in turn led to the development of snow skiing facilities at Lagganlia near Kingussie.) The main and intermediate slopes together are in excess of 500 metres in length and a cross country track undulates for a further 750 metres. There are also 3 runs of International Standard for grass skiing. Together with a complete infrastructure of practice sessions, equipment hire, ski tow, chairlift and àpres-ski, the centre provides an interesting alternative to snow skiing throughout the year.

International events are held at Hillend and there is no doubt at all that the training facilities have increased the number of Scottish skiers in Olympic and other International events.

With Hibernian in the premier league and Heart of Midlothian in the First Division, football aficionados are ensured of plenty of activity in the season.

The scene in Edinburgh on a Saturday morning before an international rugger match has to be seen to be believed. Murrayfield, the home of Scottish Rugger is one of the finest pitches in the world. There are traditionally two internationals in the early part of each year. One year the Scottish team play France and then England and the following year the matches are against Wales and Ireland.

Motor racing takes place at Ingliston, also the home of the Royal Highland Show, as well as at East Fortune, East Lothian, where the accent is on motorcycles. Also centred in East Lothian is the very much more sedate activity of pony trekking and for the esoteric, hang gliding takes place in the Pentlands and sand yachting at Dunbar.

Above: Scotland v Ireland at Murrayfield, 1977
Opposite: The Royal Commonwealth Pool, Edinburgh

In 1970 the then Edinburgh Corporation opened Meadowbank Sports Centre for the Commonwealth Games. It is now owned and operated by the City of Edinburgh

This magnificent building provides facilities for over 30 activities including archery, athletics, badminton, basketball, boxing, cricket practice, cycling, fencing, football (association), football (five-a-side), golf practice, gymnastics, handball, hockey (indoor and outdoor), judo, karate, keep fit, lacrosse, music and movement, netball, pistol shooting, rifle shooting, rock climbing, rugby, squash, table tennis, tennis, trampolining, volleyball, weight lifting, weight training, wrestling and yoga.

Indoors there are three large multi-purpose sports halls, three smaller practice halls and a number of specialist areas, i.e. a rock-climbing wall, six squash courts, a physical conditioning room, a combat room, an indoor athletic area and three range halls. Two of the sports halls can accommodate large numbers of spectators.

Outdoor facilities consist of an athletics stadium with a 400 m Tartan track, flood-lighting and accommodation for 15,000 spectators, a 250 m cycling velodrome, an athletics training area, three all-weather tennis courts, one grass and one Dri-pla area. The Dri-pla training area is also provided with flood-lighting for evening use in winter.

There are two main centres of yachting activity in the Lothians. One is at Granton Harbour where regular races are held, and the other is at the attractive village of Cramond on the Firth of Forth.

At Powderhall in Edinburgh, greyhound racing takes place as well as Speedway and regular Horse Races are held at Musselburgh, 7 miles from Edinburgh.

Left: Meadowbank Sports Centre
Photograph by courtesy of the City of Edinburgh

Dinghy racing at Cramond

COUNTRYSIDE

The Region is favoured with a diversity of coastal and countryside scenery ranging from rolling hill ranges in the South to dune coast along the Forth Estuary. There is little doubt that in terms of countryside resources Lothian has both quantity and quality. In the South are the grass and heather clad hills of the Lammermuirs, Moorfoots and Pentlands, in the West the agricultural and industrial lands of the oil shale mining industry and in the East are the agricultural landscapes and shore line of East Lothian, so rich in wildlife and recreational opportunities. The valleys of the Almond, Esk and Tyne traverse the region and are in places heavily wooded.

The international significance of Edinburgh is unquestioned, but its equally important rôle is as the heart of Lothian with a two way flow of recreational traffic, outwards towards the beaches and countryside and inwards towards the more sophisticated cultural and recreational resources of the city.

The region has valuable water resources both inland and coastal. The inland water consists largely of 37 reservoirs most of which are used for water supply or storage purposes. Certain of these reservoirs are important for wildfowl and the Department of Recreation and Leisure helps to ensure that the proper balance between conservation, recreation and water supply is maintained. Another important inland water resource is the Union Canal. Unfortunately the canal has been allowed to decline into a state of disrepair and there is little doubt that to restore it to its former condition would be costly. How-

Throughout the Region there are golf courses, bowling greens, pitch and putt courses, football, rugger and cricket pitches that are available for use. Administered by the respective District Councils they play an important part in the recreational use of urban areas. In addition one must not discount the extensive facilities that exist in the educational establishments in Lothian Reg-

ion. These facilities are used extensively by the public for training and educational purposes.

Finally, one must remember the advantages of sports not for those who take part but for those who spectate. In Lothian Region there is a wide variety of high quality spectator sport throughout the week.

ever plans are already in hand to maintain and clear the channel and towpath so that at least those parts of the canal that are suitable for recreational purposes can be used. The Union Canal is valuable as an area of slow flowing fresh water and such habitats for wildlife are rare in the region. It is important that the recreational and conservational potential of the canal are not underestimated.

The Forth Estuary is also an important area for recreation, industry and wildlife. The beaches are frequently heavily utilised by resident and visitor alike and the demand for launching and mooring sailing craft ensures that the small harbours are bustling with activity. The creation of sailing facilities can be expensive but it is essential that any new development in this most sensitive area is carefully integrated with the existence of wildlife sites of international importance.

The Pentland Hills, an area of some 50,000 acres, have a diverse land use including farming, military training, water catchment and storage, mineral extraction and forestry. Due to their accessibility and attractive landscape the hills are assuming an important role in satisfying demands for outdoor recreation. In order to integrate these pressures with the traditional land users the hills have been proposed a Regional Park where coordinated recreation and conservation planning can take place.

In West Lothian the well established Almondell and Calderwood Country Park near Livingston provides an easily accessible recreational area with good facilities for woodland and riverside walks,

picnicking and fishing in this heavily industrialised area of the region.

The John Muir Country Park near Dunbar is named after the East Lothian naturalist who was instrumental in establishing the system of National Parks in the United States. It is in its early stages of development but offers access to the coast in the vicinity of Belhaven Bay to the West of Dunbar at the mouth of the River Tyne.

Thus it will be seen that throughout the region a network of Country Parks and accessible countryside of great variety and interest has been created and is being extended. There is little doubt that with proper management and sensitive zoning in terms of both time and space the existing resources can provide a high quality of recreational facilities for the resident and visitor alike in Lothian Region. It is perhaps fortunate that much can be achieved in the countryside by thoughtful planning to improve the quality of life at very little cost to the public purse.

TRAILS

One way in which interest can be focused on a specific subject in the countryside or town is by the creation of a trail. Lothian is rich in many different types of trails. For example there are

Conservation Trails:

Blackett Association showing Edinburgh's South Side.

Nature Trails:

Throughout the Region.

Town Trails:

Haddington.

Heritage Trails:

Linlithgow and shores of the Forth.

The Paraffin Young Trail:

West Lothian.

The Real Ale Trail:

Belhaven, East Lothian.

The Department of Recreation and Leisure was instrumental in establishing two of these trails.

The Real Ale Trail was planned to show the brewing of Real Ale at the Belhaven Brewery near Dunbar. The tour visits many picturesque spots in East Lothian and luncheon includes a free glass of real ale.

The Paraffin Young Trail was created because of the tremendous interest that has been shown recently in Paraffin Young's early activities in mining shale in West Lothian and the subsequent extraction of it.

PLACES TO VISIT

EDINBURGH ZOO

To most people, a Zoo is merely a place where the public can go to look at a wide range of exotic animals. But although this type of institution offers a great deal of entertainment and amusement to both adults and children, its real function is much more important.

The Royal Zoological Society of Scotland is a charity whose income is used to study animals and wildlife from all over the world. Furthermore, it is concerned with the breeding and protection of endangered species. Hence the main function of the Zoo is educational and conservational. It also provides an unrivalled opportunity to the visitor to appreciate how important it is to safeguard animals: a zoo is not an institution which captures animals only to show them off to the public.

The Scottish National Zoological Park extends over 70 acres, laid out on grounds on the Southern slope of Corstorphine Hill. The Educational Centre is open to visitors and, with slide shows, talks and demonstrations, brings home to the public that the caging of a few animals from many different species is not an act of cruelty, but an act of charity. The Children's Farm, Aquarium, and the world famous Penguin Colony are amongst many unique and educational aspects of Edinburgh Zoo.

It is to be hoped that of the thousands of visitors who come to see the animals every year, many will learn something of lasting value.

The Penguins at Edinburgh Zoo

Edinburgh Botanic Gardens:
sculpture by Reg Butler

No. 5 Charlotte Square is the head
quarters of the National Trust for Scot
land. No. 7 is its Georgian House. It is a
town house in the North facade of Char
lotte Square, designed by Robert Adam
In 1797, John Lamont of Lamont moved
into it; in 1966, No. 7 was conveyed to
the National Trust for Scotland after the
death of the 5th Marquess of Bute.

In 1973, the National Trust for Scotland
decided to convert the basement, ground
and first floors into a Georgian show
piece. Most of the furniture, as far a
possible, is in the style of the period
1790-1810, which is to say, that of George
III.

The visitor may reconstruct for himsel
an idea of what life was like in the New
Town during its earliest years; indeed
when the sounds of masons and carpenter
could be heard constructing the "second
New Town" a little further to the North

THE ROYAL BOTANIC GARDEN

In the Northern end of the city, the Royal
Botanic Garden has a world-famous rock
garden, an enormous range of exotic
plants and, at the summit, the Scottish
National Gallery of Modern Art in
Inverleith House. In its way, the Botanic
Garden encapsulates the varying degrees
of naturalness and artificiality of the city
and countryside: from countryside to
garden, and finally to pure art.

INGLISTON

The Royal Highland Show takes place annually at Ingliston during the third week of June. Like its counterparts in Norfolk and elsewhere, the show is predominantly agricultural but with interesting sidelines. Most of the latter are provided by the large number of commercial organizations at work throughout the country; there is also a chance to indulge in some serious winetasting. One of the central attractions of the show for those who are not primarily there "on business" is the equestrian events.

An agricultural centre has recently been established by the Royal Highland and Agricultural Society of Scotland, proprietors of Ingliston, and organisers of the Royal Highland Show and other events. This venture has been supported by more than 40 other organizations.

Development in the showground includes a motor racing circuit which is constantly in use, and the MacRobert Pavilion, a permanent feature, available for conferences, banquets and other assorted items during the year.

Ingliston itself, within a mile of Edinburgh Airport, extends to 86 acres of parkland, with another 200 acres of fields used for car parks. It is just within the city boundary on the western outskirts.

The Royal Highland Show, Ingliston

BARNS NESS GEOLOGICAL TRAIL

At Barns Ness, and along the $2\frac{1}{2}$ mile stretch of coast from White Sands Beach to Thornton Loch, can be seen the sedimentary rocks laid down in the Palaeozoic Era. These limestone rocks date from 280-345 million years ago, and are rich in fossils. This stretch of land was gifted to the local authority by the Associated Portland and Cement Manufacturers Ltd.

A geological trail has been laid out amongst the limestones outcropping on the foreshore, and is a good example of the cooperation between governmental and commercial bodies.

Shore Fauna is varied; periwinkles, limpets and whelks may be examined. Seaweeds are particularly rich in this Dunbar area of the Firth of Forth. Since there are numerous pools between tidemarks, and creeks and crevices offering many different combinations of light and shade, there is a luxuriant growth of several species of seaweed normally belonging to deeper water.

For the birdwatcher, the South East coast of Scotland contains a wide variety of birdlife. The Gannets from the nearby Bass Rock colony can be observed diving for fish. Many other varieties of birds are in evidence, including the Kestrel making its frequent visits; off-shore Razor bills and Guillemots mingle with the several different families of Terns which fish closer inland. During the late summer months the variety and numbers of birds increase at Barns Ness, for the area attracts some of the migrants from the very northern reaches of Europe heading towards the Equator.

Razorbill	Yellow Hammer
Guillemots	Starling
Redshank	Gannet
Tern (Common,	Eider Duck
Arctic, Roseate,	Shelduck
Sandwich, and Little)	Curlew
Oyster-catcher	Turnstone
Ringed Plover	Skylark
Pied Wagtail	Greenfinch
Meadow Pipit	Linnet
Gold Finch	Wren
Dunnock	Reed Bunting

Kestrel	Short-Eared Owl
Shrike (Woodchat,	Swift
Great Grey, Red	Redwing
Backed)	Merlin
Barred Warbler	Longtailed Duck
Lesser White-throat	Goldeneye
Pied Flycatcher	Red-Throated Diver
Redstart	Blackcap
Bar-tailed Godwit	Garden Warbler
Curlew Sandpiper	Wryneck

Black Redstart	Fieldfare
Golden Plover	Merganser
Little Stint	Scoter
Swallow	Grebe
Sandmartin	Red breasted
Snow Bunting	Flycatcher

In order to enjoy this rich natural life the building of a camp site was discussed in 1967. At present, it operates for 80 units and is positioned at the foot of the 25 foot raised beach lying along the southern fringe of the coast. It has been cunningly positioned so as not to disturb the natural beauty of the local landscape. It is run by the Camping Club of Great Britain and was built with the help of a government grant determined by the Countryside (Scotland) Act.

THE BASS ROCK

The Bass is a noticeable landmark off the coast of Lothian. It stands at the entrance to the Firth of Forth, and is situated $3\frac{1}{4}$ miles ENE of North Berwick, $1\frac{1}{4}$ miles from the coast. One mile in circumference, the Rock rises 350 feet above sea level and was formed of igneous rock, phonolite (clinkstone), about 320 million years ago.

It is difficult to discern the origin of the Rock's name. The name is probably Celtic, meaning a rock of conical shape. There is a similar word in Norse and Icelandic. Some, however, consider the name to come from the Gaelic "Bathais" signifying forehead. Others trace it to Bass, a man mentioned in the Scots chronicle "The Book of Lecain".

Tantallon Castle and the Bass Rock

The history of the Bass Rock is of some interest as the rock, due to its strategic position in the Firth of Forth, changed hands regularly. Saint Baldred, disciple of Saint Mungo, grandson of Loth, is said to have been the first settler on the Bass. He died in 607. Traditionally, the Bass was granted to the Lauder family by Malcolm III in the 11th century. In 1405, Prince James, son of Robert III, was sent to a refuge there before being taken to France. He never reached France and spent 19 years in English captivity.

In 1671, the Bass Rock was sold by Sir Alexander Ramsay to the Duke of Lauderdale. Lauderdale wanted it in order to imprison Covenanters there. Sir Hew Dalrymple, 1st Baronet, bought the Rock in 1706 and it remains in the hands of his descendants.

There is a light house on the Rock, built in 1902, and the Tower stands 67 feet high.

However, it is not its history which has made the Bass Rock famous. It is the Gannet. The bird has been there at least since the seventh century. Two thirds of the world's gannets are hatched on the cliff ledges of 13 gannetries in the British Isles of which Saint Kilda is the largest and the Bass Rock the most famous.

From North Berwick harbour, there are regular pleasure boat sailings around the Bass in summer. Although it is possible for genuine naturalists to obtain permission to land, the best views of the seabird colonies can be got from the boat sailing under the crags of the Rock.

Flowering Plants of the Bass Rock

Creeping Buttercup
Common Scurvy
Grass
Red Campion
Dark Green Mouse-
ear Chickweed
Little Mouse-ear
Chickweed
Blinks
Hastate Orache
Dove's-foot Cranesbill
Spring Vetch
Starwort
Sorrel
Stinging Nettle
Sea Pink
Cleavers
Groundsel
Welted Thistle
March Thistle
Sow Thistle
Red Fescue
Annual Poa
Rough Poa

Soft Brome
Yorkshire Foy
Hedge Mustard
Eastern Rocket
Sea Campion
Sea Beet
Tree Mallow
White Clover
Rosebay Willowherb
Persicaria
Curled Dock
Small Nettle
Ribwort
Elder
Slender Thistle
Spear Thistle
Creeping Thistle
Dandelion
Sheep's Fescue
Meadow-Grass
Cock's-Foot
Wild Oat
Common Kent-grass

Breeding Birds of the Bass Rock

Gannet (Solan
Goose) wing-span
36 ins.
Fulmar: 18½ ins.
Shag or Green
Cormorant: 30 ins.
Lesser Blackheaded
Gull: 21 ins.
Herring Gull: 23 ins.
Razorbill: 16 ins.
Puffin: 12 ins.
Hedge Sparrow:
5 ins.

Rock Pipit: 6 ins.
Black browed
Albatross: 36 ins. An
occasional visitor
since 1967, it has not
yet found a mate on
the Bass Rock.
Kittiwake: 16 ins.
Guillemot: 16½ ins.
Blackbird: 10 ins.
Linnet: 5 ins.

Right: Red Campion

Left: Common Scurvey Grass

Gannet (Solan Goose), wingspan 36 ins.

Albatross, wingspan 36 ins.

JOHN MUIR COUNTRY PARK

Dunbar is reputed to be in the sunniest place in Scotland. It is also the birthplace of John Muir. In 1849 he emigrated with his parents to America and became famous as an explorer and naturalist.

In America, John Muir inspired the setting up of the Yosemite and Sequoia Parks, hence pioneering the United States National Park system. In his memory, the John Muir Country Park has been established at Dunbar. It is an area of land set aside for the conservation of natural surroundings.

Belhaven Beach, 700 yards wide and one mile in length, offers an enormous expanse dedicated to the pursuit of pleasurable activities: horse riding, sand yachting and surfing. Sea fishing and walking may be enjoyed by those not so athletically inclined.

At the east end of the Park lies the ruin of Dunbar Castle. It guards the entrance to the harbour still, although Cromwell had part of the castle destroyed to provide stone for a herring harbour. Today, its cobbled quays act as shelter for pleasure craft.

The John Muir Country Park helps to maintain the ancient town of Dunbar and its surroundings as an important tourist centre. The splendour and simplicity of the natural environment contrasts with the charm and quietness of the town.

GAZETTEER

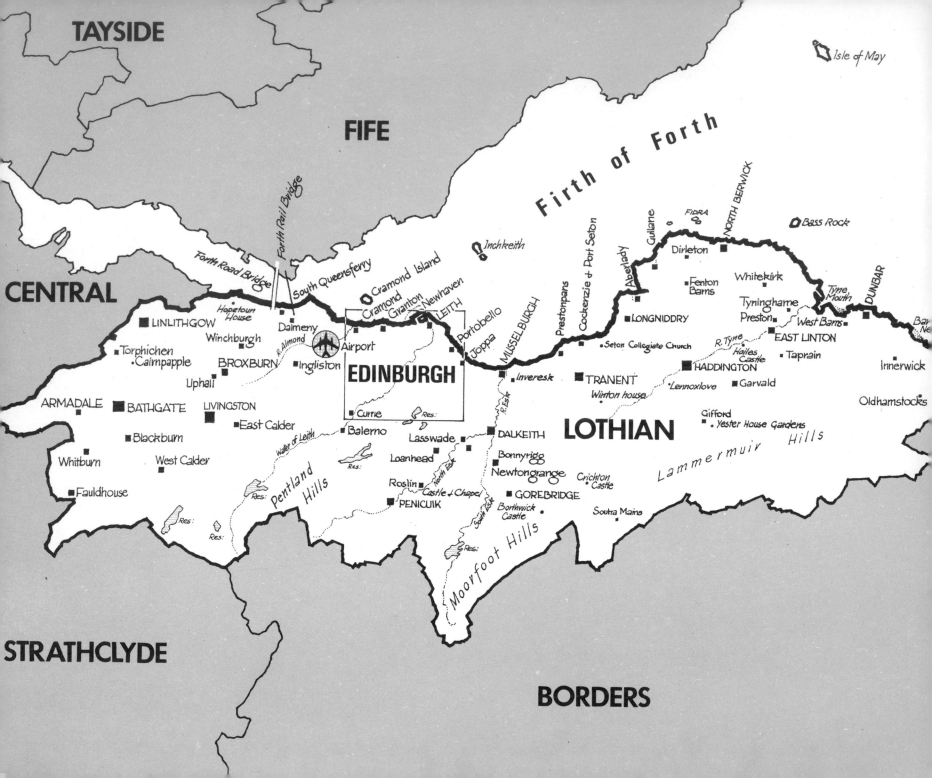

Queen Mary's Harp (The National Museum of Antiquities)

MUSEUMS

EDINBURGH WAX MUSEUM

High Street, Edinburgh. Tel. 031-226 4445
Open: Easter–October   1000–1900

HUNTLY HOUSE

Canongate, Edinburgh. Tel. 031-556 5813
Open: Mondays–Saturdays
                                  1000–1700

LADY STAIR'S HOUSE

Off the Lawnmarket in the Royal Mile,
Edinburgh.   Tel. 031-225 8160
Open: Mondays–Saturdays   1000–1700

MUSEUM OF CHILDHOOD

High Street, Edinburgh.
                          Tel. 031-556 5447
Open: Mondays–Saturdays   1000–1700

MYRETON MOTOR MUSEUM

Woodbine Cottage, Myreton, Aberlady,
East Lothian.   Tel. Aberlady 288
Open: Easter–October   1000–1800
Also open October–Easter at weekends
                                  1000–1700

NATIONAL MUSEUM OF ANTIQUITIES OF SCOTLAND

Queen Street, Edinburgh.
                          Tel. 031-556 8921
Open: Mondays–Saturdays   1000–1700
        Sundays   1400–1700

ROYAL SCOTTISH MUSEUM

Chambers Street, Edinburgh.
                          Tel. 031-225 7534
Open: Mondays–Saturdays   1000–1700
        Sundays   1400–1700

RUSHBROOK AND BRAID WOOD MUSEUM

McDonald Road Fire Station, Edinburgh.
                          Tel. 031-229 7222
Open: Guided tours may be arranged by
        contacting the Central Office at the
        above number.

THE RUSSELL COLLECTION OF HARPSICHORDS

St. Cecilia's Hall, Cowgate, Edinburgh.
                          Tel. 031-667 1011
Open: Saturdays only   1400–1700
Collection of early musical instruments.

ST. CUTHBERT'S CO-OPERATIVE COACH BUILDINGS AND STABLES

Gardners Crescent, Edinburgh.
                          Tel. 031-229 2424
Open: Visits by special arrangement.
        Apply in writing to: The Manager,
        at the above address.

THE SCOTTISH NATIONAL WAR MEMORIAL

Crown Square,
The Castle, Edinburgh.
                          Tel. 031-226 7393
Open: May–October
        Mondays–Saturdays   0930–1800
        Sundays   1100–1800
        November–April
        Mondays–Saturdays   0930–1630
        Sundays   1230–1630

SCOTTISH UNITED SERVICES MUSEUM

Crown Square,
The Castle, Edinburgh.
                          Tel. 031-226 6907
Open: May–October
        Mondays–Saturdays   0930–1800
        Sundays   1100–1800
        November–April
        Mondays–Saturdays   0930–1630
        Sundays   1230–1630

CANONGATE TOLBOOTH

163 Canongate, Edinburgh.
Tel. 031-556 5813
Open: Mondays–Saturdays   1000–1700

TRANSPORT MUSEUM

Lothian Region Transport Bus Works at
Shrubhill, Leith Walk.
Open: Mondays to Fridays   1000–1700

QUEENSFERRY MUSEUM

Council Offices, High Street, South
Queensferry.
Entry by appointment. Tel. 031-331 1590

LINLITHGOW CANAL MUSEUM

Manse Basin, Linlithgow, West Lothian.
Open: Easter–October
       Saturdays & Sundays   1400–1700

NORTH BERWICK MUSEUM

School Road, North Berwick, East
Lothian.
Open: Easter–24th September
       Mondays–Saturdays   1000–1300
                        and 1400–1700
       Sundays   1400–1700

ART GALLERIES

ROYAL SCOTTISH ACADEMY

The Mound, Princes Street, Edinburgh.
Open: Mondays–Saturdays   1000–2100
       Sundays   1400–1700
Tel. 031-225 6671

THE NATIONAL GALLERY OF SCOTLAND

The Mound, Edinburgh (behind Royal
Scottish Academy)
Open: Mondays–Saturdays   1000–1700
       Sundays   1400–1700
Tel. 031-556 8942

SCOTTISH NATIONAL GALLERY OF MODERN ART

Inverleith House, Royal Botanic Garden,
Inverleith Row, Edinburgh.
Open: Mondays–Saturdays 100–1800
       (In winter, 1000–1 hr. before sun-
       set)
       Sundays, 1400–1800
       (In winter, 1300–1600 or 1 hr be-
       fore sunset.)
Tel. 031-332 3754

SCOTTISH NATIONAL PORTRAIT GALLERY

Queen Street, Edinburgh.
Open: Mondays–Saturdays   1000–1700
       Sundays   1400–1700
Tel. 031-556 8921

SCOTTISH ARTS COUNCIL GALLERY

19 Charlotte Square, Edinburgh.
Open: Mondays–Saturdays   1000–1800
       Sundays   1400–1800
Tel. 031-226 6051

FRUIT MARKET GALLERY

29 Market Street, Edinburgh.
Open: Mondays–Saturdays   1000–1730
Tel. 031-226 5781

THEATRES

CHURCHILL THEATRE

Morningside Road
Edinburgh
Tel. 031-447 7597

LEITH THEATRE

Ferry Road
Edinburgh
Tel. 031-554 7295

USHER HALL

Lothian Road
Edinburgh
Tel. 031-228 1155

KING'S THEATRE

Leven Street
Edinburgh
Tel. 031-229 1201

ROYAL LYCEUM THEATRE

Grindlay Street
Edinburgh
Tel. 031-229 9697

LYCEUM LITTLE THEATRE

Cambridge Street
Edinburgh
Tel. 031-229 1231

TRAVERSE THEATRE

112 West Bow
Edinburgh
Tel. 031-226 2633

BRUNTON HALL

High Street
Musselburgh
East Lothian
Tel. 031-665 3711

LIVINGSTON MEWS THEATRE

Howden Park Centre
Livingston
West Lothian
Tel. Livingston 33634

Craigmillar Castle

BUILDINGS OF HISTORIC INTEREST

CASTLES   PALACES

CRAIGMILLAR CASTLE

A68. 3 miles South West of Edinburgh City Centre.
Open: April–September

Mondays–Saturdays	0930–1900
Sundays	1400–1900
October–March	
Mondays–Saturdays	0930–1600
Sundays	1400–1600

CRICHTON CASTLE

Situated South-South West of Pathhead, Midlothian
Open: April–September

Mondays–Saturdays	0930–1900
Sundays	1400–1900
October–March	0930–1600

Closed Fridays, October to May

DIRLETON CASTLE

A198. 7 miles West of North Berwick, East Lothian.
Open: April–September
Mondays–Saturdays	0930–1900
Sundays	1400–1900
October–March
Mondays–Saturdays	0930–1600
Sundays	1400–1600

EDINBURGH CASTLE

Castle Rock, top of Royal Mile, Edinburgh
Open: May–October
Mondays–Saturdays	0930–1715
Sundays	1100–1715
November–April
Mondays–Saturdays	0930–1620
Sundays	1230–1531

HAILES CASTLE

Off A1. 5 miles East of Haddington, East Lothian
Open: April–September
Mondays–Saturdays	0930–1900
Sundays	1400–1900
October–March
Mondays–Saturdays	0930–1600
Sundays	1400–1600

PALACE OF HOLYROODHOUSE

Canongate, Royal Mile, Edinburgh
Tel. 031-556 1847
Open: May–October
Mondays–Saturdays	0930–1715
Sundays	1100–1715
November–April
Mondays–Saturdays	0930–1645
Sundays	1230–1645
(The Palace is closed during Royal and State Visits.)

LAURISTON CASTLE

Off A90 at Cramond Road South, 4 miles West North West of Edinburgh City Centre
Open: April–October daily except Friday
Castle: 1100–1300 & 1400–1700
Grounds: 1100–dusk
November–March 1400–1700
Saturdays and Sundays only

LINLITHGOW PALACE

Linlithgow, West Lothian
Open: April–September
Mondays–Saturdays	0930–1900
Sundays	1400–1900
October–March
Mondays–Saturdays	0930–1600
Sundays	1400–1600

ROSSLYN CASTLE

Off A703. $7\frac{1}{2}$ miles South of Edinburgh
Roslin Midlothian   Tel. 031-440 2097
Open: Daily 1000–1700

TANTALLON CASTLE

A198, 3 miles East of North Berwick, East Lothian
Open: April–September
Mondays–Saturdays	0930–1900
Sundays	1400–1900
October–March
Mondays–Saturdays	0930–1600
Sundays	1400–1600

Winton House

HISTORIC HOUSES

THE BINNS

4 miles East of Linlithgow
West Lothian   Tel. Philpstoun 255
Open: Easter to September
Daily except Fridays	1400–1730

GEORGIAN HOUSE

No. 7 Charlotte Square
Edinburgh   Tel. 031-226 5922
Open: April–September
	1000–1700
Sundays	1400–1700
October–March
Saturdays	1000–1700
Sundays	1400–1700

HOPETOUN HOUSE

South Queensferry, West Lothian
Tel. 031-331 1546 or 031-331 2451
Open: May–September, daily 1100–1730

WINTON HOUSE

On B6355, 6 miles South West of
Haddington   Tel. Pencaitland 340222
Open: by prior arrangement, to parties
       only or people very specially in-
       terested (Sir David Ogilvy)

Kirk of the Greyfriars

HISTORIC CHURCHES

HIGH KIRK OF ST. GILES

Royal Mile, Edinburgh
Open: Mondays–Saturdays   1000–1700

KIRK OF THE GREYFRIARS

Greyfriars Place, South end of George IV
Bridge, Edinburgh
Open: May–September   1000–1200
                           1400–1530
Sundays—open for services only.

ROSSLYN CHAPEL

Roslin, Midlothian
Open: Easter–October
      Mondays–Saturdays   1000–1300
                           1400–1700

ST. MARY'S PARISH CHURCH

Haddington, East Lothian
Open: April–September   1000–2000
      September–April
      Keys available from Lodge House.

ST. MICHAEL'S PARISH CHURCH

South Shore of Loch, Linlithgow, West
Lothian
Open: 1000–1200, 1400–1600
      (Except Thursday)
      Sundays   1000–1200

SETON COLLEGIATE CHURCH

Situated off the A198 13 miles East of
Edinburgh, East Lothian
Open: April–September
      Mondays–Saturdays   0930–1900
      Sundays   1400–1900
      October–March

Mondays–Saturdays   0930–1600
Sundays   1400–1600

TORPHICHEN PRECEPTORY

B792. 5 miles South-South West of
Linlithgow, West Lothian
Open: April–September
      Mondays–Saturdays   0930–1900
      Sundays   1400–1900
      October–March
      Mondays–Saturdays   0930–1600
      Sundays   1400–1600

WHITEKIRK

On A198. 5 miles South East of North
Berwick, East Lothian
                   Tel. East Linton 294
Visitors may be conducted round the
Church by arrangement with the Minister.

DUNGLASS COLLEGIATE CHURCH

At Cockburnspath, off A1, 8 miles South
East of Dunbar
Open: All reasonable times

ABERLADY CHURCH

In Aberlady, A198, 7 miles South West
of North Berwick
Open: All reasonable times

GIFFORD CHURCH

In Gifford, B6369, 5 miles South-South
East of Haddington
Open: All reasonable times

CANONGATE KIRK

Canongate, Royal Mile, Edinburgh
Open: on request. Apply the Manse,
Reid's Court, near the Church

MAGDALEN CHAPEL

Cowgate, off Grassmarket, Edinburgh
Open: Fridays   0900–1700

ST. MARY'S CATHEDRAL

Palmerston Place, Edinburgh
Open: All reasonable times

Preston Mill

OTHER PLACES OF INTEREST

OUTLOOK TOWER AND CAMERA OBSCURA

Castlehill, Edinburgh
Open Daily,   0930–1730
Tel. 031-226 3709

JOHN KNOX'S HOUSE

High Street, Royal Mile, Edinburgh
Open: Mondays–Saturdays   1000–1700
Tel. 031-556 6961

ACHESON HOUSE

(Scottish Craft Centre)
140 Canongate, Royal Mile, Edinburgh
Open: Mondays–Saturdays   1000–1700
Tel. 031-556 8136

SCOTT MONUMENT

Princes Street, Edinburgh
Open: Mondays–Saturdays   0900–1800

ROYAL OBSERVATORY

Blackford Hill, Edinburgh
Details of visits and tours supplied on
request.
Tel. 031-667 3321

SCOTTISH RECORD OFFICE

HM General Register House, East Princes
Street and West Register House, Charlotte
Square, Edinburgh
Open: Mondays–Thursdays   0930–1630
       Saturdays   0930–1600
Tel. General Register House 031-556 6585
     West Register House   031-226 5101

CALTON HILL AND NELSON MONUMENT

Off Regent Road, Edinburgh
Monument open: April–September
     Mondays–Saturdays   1000–1900
     October–March
     Mondays–Saturdays   1000–1500

PARLIAMENT HOUSE

High Street, Edinburgh
Open: Tuesdays–Fridays   1000–1630
       Saturdays   1000–1430

CITY CHAMBERS

High Street, Edinburgh
Open to visitors, Mondays–Fridays
1000–1500 when Council business permits.

NATIONAL LIBRARY OF SCOTLAND

George IV Bridge, Edinburgh
Open: (Reading Room)
     Mondays–Fridays   0930–2030
     Saturdays   0930–1300
     (Exhibition)
     Mondays–Fridays   0930–1700
     Saturdays   0930–1300

PRESTON MILL

Off A1 at East Linton, 6 miles West of
Dunbar
Open: Mondays–Saturdays   1000–1230
                   and 1400–1930
     Sundays   1400–1930
     (closed 1630 October–March)

THE FORTH BRIDGES

Queensferry, 10 miles West of Edinburgh the Forth Road Bridge, opened in 1964, is one of the longest suspension bridges in Europe, over 1½ miles long. It stands near the famous Victorian rail bridge of 1883-90, which carries the rail-link to the Highlands.

Cairnpapple Hill

ANCIENT MONUMENTS

CAIRNPAPPLE HILL

Originally, a Neolithic sanctuary, built over in the early Bronze Age (circa 1800 BC), it became a monumental open-air temple, with a circle of stone and an enclosing ditch. This was later built over as a Bronze Age cairn (circa 1500 BC). The plot is situated near Bathgate off the B792.

Other notable field monuments can be seen at:

THE HOPES

South of Gifford on the B6355

THE CHESTERS

South of Aberlady off the B1377

SOUTRA AISLE

Off the A6137 north of Huntershall

CRICHTON MAINS

Off the B6367 near Crichton

CASTLELAW

Off the A702 near the Hillend Ski Slope

DALMAHOY

Near Balerno on the A70

CASTLE GREG

On the B7000 south-east of West Calder

The Pentlands from Harlaw Moor

COUNTRY PARKS/ GARDENS/NATURE TRAILS

PENTLAND HILLS

Ranger Service/Further Information Countryside Information Centre, Hillend Park, Biggar Road, Edinburgh
Open: April–September
Mondays–Fridays	0900–1700
Saturdays 0900–1000;	1600–1700
Sundays	1000–1300
October–March	
Mondays–Fridays	0900–1700

ALMONDELL COUNTRY PARK

East Calder
West Lothian
Ranger Service/Further Information
Tel. Mid Calder 882254

BARNS NESS AND WHITESANDS

Off A1. 3½ miles south east of Dunbar
East Lothian
For further information contact:
East Lothian Tourist Information Centre
Tel. Dunbar 63353

BEECRAIGS COUNTRY PARK

Bathgate Hills
3 miles south of Linlithgow, West Lothian
Ranger Service/Further Information
Tel. Mid Calder 882254

THE BINNS

Off A904. 4 miles east of Linlithgow, West Lothian

Open: Easter–September   1000–1900
For further information Tel. Philpstoun 255

DALKEITH PARK

Dalkeith
For further information contact Midlothian Department of Recreation and Leisure
Tel. 031-440 0352

HOPETOUN HOUSE NATURE TRAIL

West of South Queensferry, West Lothian
Open: May–September   1330–1730
    Daily except Thursdays and Fridays
For further information Tel. 031-331 1546 or 031-331 2451

JOHN MUIR COUNTRY PARK

Belhaven, East Lothian
Ranger Service/Further Information
Tel. East Linton 556

YELLOWCRAIG NATURE TRAIL

Off the A198. 2 miles west of North Berwick, East Lothian
Ranger Service/Further Information
Tel. Aberlady 265

WATER OF LEITH WALKWAY, EDINBURGH

Slateford to Juniper Green
For further information contact City of

Edinburgh District Council Planning Department, 18 Market Street, Edinburgh.
Tel. 031-225 2424

CRAMOND VILLAGE

5 miles North West of Edinburgh city centre, on the shores of the Firth of Forth. Picturesque walks along Forth and River Almond, Roman fort etc.
Conducted walks around village from Cramond Kirk, June–September; Sundays 1500 hours.

GARDENS

INVERESK LODGE GARDEN

Situated 7 miles east of Edinburgh
Open: All year
    Monday–Friday   1000–1630
    Sundays (May–September)
        1400–1700

MALLENY GARDENS

Situated off the A70. 7½ miles south west of Edinburgh
Open: May–September   1000–170

PRINCES STREET GARDENS

Edinburgh
Open: All year
    Summer   0800–Sunse
    Winter   0800–Dus

ROYAL BOTANIC GARDEN

Inverleith Row Edinburgh
Open: Summer: Monday–Saturday 0900
    Sunday 1100 to one hour befor Sunset
    Winter: Monday–Saturday 0900
    Sunday 1100 to Dusk

SAUGHTON ROSE GARDEN

Corner of Gorgie Road and Balgree Road, Edinburgh
Open: All year
    Summer   0800–Sunse
    Winter   0800–Dus

SUNTRAP

Situated off the A8 at Gogarburn 6 mile west of Edinburgh
Open: Monday–Friday   0900–170
    Saturday   0900–120

EDINBURGH ZOO

(The Royal Zoological Society o Scotland) Murrayfield, Edinburgh (en

ance from Corstorphine Road A8)
pen: April–September   0900–1900
       October–March   0900–1700
el. 031-334 9171

T. MARY'S PLEASANCE

addington House, Sidegate, Haddington,
ast Lothian (Haddington Garden Trust)
pen: All reasonable times

PORTS CENTRES
PORT AND RECREATION

IEADOWBANK SPORTS
ENTRE

9 London Road, Edinburgh
. major leisure complex offering facilities
or upwards of thirty sports for club and
dividual participation. Club, National
nd International events are held here. For
etails and bookings   Tel. 031-661 5351

JACK KANE CENTRE

53 Niddrie Marischal Road, Edinburgh
This centre offers facilities for a large
selection of indoor and outdoor sports.
For details and bookings:
Tel. 031-669 0404

NORTH BERWICK SPORTS CENTRE

Grange Road, North Berwick, East
Lothian
Indoor facilities for Badminton, Squash,
Table Tennis, Basketball, Billiards, Bowl-
ing etc. For details and bookings:
Tel. 0620 3454

BONNYRIGG SPORTS CENTRE

Lasswade High School, Eskdale Drive,
Bonnyrigg, Midlothian
This new centre offers facilities for a
selection of indoor and outdoor sports.
For details and bookings:
Tel. 031-660 2117

SKI-ING
HILLEND SKI CENTRE

Biggar Road, Edinburgh
One of the world's largest Artificial Ski
Slopes, 400 metres with two runs. Chairlift and Ski Tow. Instruction and Equipment Hire. Competitions and Champion-
ship events from time to time. Facilities
for cross country and grass ski-ing.
Tel. 031-445 4433/4/5

RIDING AND
PONY TREKKING

Recently revised list of Riding and
Trekking Centres attached.

HORSE RACING

Race meetings are held at Musselburgh
Race Course, East Lothian. Further
information from: Mr. W. McHarg,
Racecourse Office, Whitletts Road, Ayr.
Tel. 0292 64179

MOTOR RACING

Race meetings are held at Ingliston,
Newbridge, Midlothian on Sundays, ap-
proxy once a month between April and
October. Further information and tickets
from: Scotcircuit, National Bank Chambers, Duns, Berwickshire.
Tel. 036-12-3724

GREYHOUND RACING

Powderhall Stadium, Beaverhall Road,
Edinburgh.
Race meetings two or three evenings a
week all year round. For dates and times
contact Stadium: Tel. 031-556 8141

GOLF

There are excellent facilities for golf in the
Lothian Region with 40 courses, including
the world famous Muirfield. Some offer
club and caddy car hire and have resident
Professionals. Information from Tourist
Information Centres or Departments of
Recreation & Leisure.

SKATING AND CURLING

Murrayfield Ice Rink, Riversdale Crescent,
Edinburgh. Open from August to June,
mainly for skating—equipment can be
hired—but also used for clubs' curling
sessions during the winter months.
Tel. 031-337 6933

FOOTBALL

There are three professional clubs in Edinburgh: Hibernian F.C. who play at Easter Road Park, Tel. 031-661 2159; Heart of Midlothian F.C. at Tynecastle Park, Tel. 031-337 6132 and Meadowbank Thistle F.C. at Meadowbank Sports Centre, Tel. 031-661 5351. Details of matches are given in the local press. There are numerous local clubs throughout the Region.

RUGBY

Rugby is a popular game with many teams competing in the autumn and winter. The highlights of the rugby year are the internationals played at Murrayfield, Edinburgh, the headquarters of the Scottish Rugby Union.   Tel. 031-337 2346

BOWLING

There are numerous bowling greens and bowling clubs in the Region. Details of facilities are available from Tourist Information Centres or Departments of Recreation & Leisure.

SWIMMING

There are six indoor swimming pools in Edinburgh as well as the Royal Commonwealth Pool and Sauna at Dalkeith Road.
Tel. 031-667 7211
There are also swimming pools at a number of other centres in the Region, including open-air pools at the seaside resorts of North Berwick and Dunbar, and an open-air pool at Portobello, Edinburgh which has excellent spectator accommodation and a wave-making machine.

TENNIS

Edinburgh has one of the finest tennis grounds in Britain at Craiglockhart Tennis Centre, 177 Colinton Road.
Tel. 031-443 2701
There are 12 all-weather and 5 grass courts; also facilities for squash and a games hall and catering facilities. There are also many other public tennis courts in all parts of the City where rackets and balls may be hired. Similar facilities are available at other centres in the Region. Further information from Tourist Information Centres or Departments of Recreation & Leisure.

YACHTING

There are a number of sailing clubs on the Firth of Forth and frequent yacht races are held.

FISHING, GOLF, AND CAMPING FACILITIES

For information, contact Department of Recreation & Leisure, Lothian Regional Council, 40 Torpichen Street, Edinburgh.
Tel. 031-229 9292
Information of local sports facilities may be obtained from:

CITY OF EDINBURGH DISTRICT COUNCIL

Recreation Department
27 York Place,
Edinburgh   Tel. 031-225 2424

MIDLOTHIAN DISTRICT COUNCIL

Recreation & Leisure Department
Municipal Buildings
Clerk Street
Loanhead, Midlothian   Tel. 031-440 0352

WEST LOTHIAN DISTRICT COUNCIL

Leisure & Recreation Department
Old County Buildings
Linlithgow, West Lothian
Tel. Linlithgow 3121

EAST LOTHIAN DISTRICT COUNCIL

Leisure, Recreation & Tourism Department
Brunton Hall
Musselburgh, East Lothian
Tel. 031-665 3711

LOTHIAN REGIONAL COUNCIL

Department of Recreation & Leisure
40 Torpichen Street
Edinburgh   Tel. 031-229 9292